David Christie Murray

The making of a novelist

an experiment in autobiography

David Christie Murray

The making of a novelist
an experiment in autobiography

ISBN/EAN: 9783337032494

Printed in Europe, USA, Canada, Australia, Japan

Cover: Foto ©Thomas Meinert / pixelio.de

More available books at **www.hansebooks.com**

THE
MAKING OF A NOVELIST

AN EXPERIMENT IN AUTOBIOGRAPHY

BY
DAVID CHRISTIE MURRAY

TO

J. M. BARRIE

PREFACE

EVERY man who writes about himself is, on the face of the matter, obnoxious to the suspicion which haunts the daily pathway of the Bore. To talk of self and not be offensive demands an art which is not always given to man. And yet we are always longing to get near each other and to understand each other; and in default of a closer communion with our living fellows we take to our bosoms the shadows of fiction and the stage. If the real man could be presented to us by any writer of his own history we should all hail him with enthusiasm.

Pepys, of course, came nearer than anybody else; but this is only because he wrote for his own reading and meant to keep himself a secret. Dickens exquisitely veils and unveils his own personality and career in *Copperfield*, and scores of smaller writers have done the same thing in fiction to our great pleasure. But to set down boldly, openly, and as a fact for general publication the things of one's own doing, saying, and thinking is an impertinence whose only justification can be found in the public approval. If Pepys had written his Diary for publication he would have been left to oblivion as a driveller. But we surprise the man's secret, we see what he never meant to show us, the peering jackdaw instinct is satisfied; and we feel, besides, a certain sense of humorous pity and affectionate disdain which the man himself, had we known him in life as we know him in his book, could never have excited. Rousseau, to me, is flatly intolerable, because he meant to tell the world what every man should have the decency to hide.

The perfect autobiography is yet to seek, and will probably never be written. A partial solution of a difficulty is offered in this experimental booklet. It is offered without diffidence, because it is offered in perfect modesty. I have tried to show how one particular novelist was made; where he got some of his experiences, and in what varying fashions the World and Fate have tried to teach him his business. It has been my effort to do this in the least egotistical and the most straightforward fashion. The narrative is quite informal and wanders where it will; but in its serial publication it received marked favour from an indulgent public, and I like to give it an equal chance of permanence with the rest of my writings, which I trust will not convey the notion that I covet a too-exaggerated longevity. Should the public favour continue, the field of experience is wide; and I may repeat Dick Swiveller's saying to Mr. Quilp—'There is plenty more in the shop this comes from.'

THE
MAKING OF A NOVELIST

I

ONLY a day or two ago I found myself arrested on my eastward way along the Strand by the hand of a friend upon my shoulder. We chatted for a minute or two, and I found that I was in front of Lipscombe's window. A ball of cork, which has had a restless time of it for many years, was dodging up and down the limits of a glass shade, tossed by a jet of water. The sight of it carried me back twenty years in a flash.

In the year 1872 I came to London, as

many young men had done before me, without funds, without friends, and without employment, trusting, with the happy-go-lucky disposition of youth, to the chapter of accidents. For some time the accidents were all unfavourable, and there came a morning when I owned nothing in the world but the clothes I stood in. I found myself that morning very tired, very hungry, very down in the mouth, staring at the cork ball on the jet of water under the glass shade, and drearily likening it to my own mental condition, flung hither and thither, drenched, rolled over, lifted and dropped by a caprice beyond the power of resistance. It was at this mournful moment that I found my first friend in London. The story of that event shall be told hereafter. What I want to say now is that the sight of that permanent show in Lipscombe's window made me younger for a minute by a score of years, and opened my mind to such a rush of recollections that I determined then and there to put my memories on paper.

I am not such an egotist as to suppose my experiences to be altogether unique; but I know them to be curious and in places surprising. Adventures, as Mr. Disraeli said a good many years ago, are to the adventurous, and in a smallish kind of way I have sought and found enough to stock the lives of a thousand stay-at-homes. At the first blush it would not appear to the outside observer that the literary life is likely to be fruitful in adventure; but in the circle of my own acquaintance there are a good many men who have found it so.

In the city of Prague the most astonishing encounters pass for every-day incidents. In these days of universal enlightenment nobody needs to be told that Prague is the capital of Bohemia. There is a note that rings false in the very name of that happy country now. Its traditions have been vulgarised by people who have never passed its borders. All sorts of charlatans have soiled its history with ignoble use, and the very centre and citadel of its capital has an air of being built of gingerbread. In point of fact, though its inhabitants are sparser than they once were, and its occasional guests of distinction fewer, the place itself is as real as ever it was. I have lived in it for a quarter of a century, and, without vanity, may claim to know it as well as any man alive.

Eight or ten years ago I was sitting in the Savage Club in the company of four distinguished men of letters. One was the editor of a London daily, and he was talking rather too humbly, as I thought, about his own career.

'I do not suppose,' he said, 'that any man in my present position has experienced in London the privations I knew when I first came here. I went hungry for three days, twenty years back, and for three nights I slept in the Park.'

One of the party turned to me. 'You cap that, Christie?'

I answered, 'Four nights on the Embankment. Four days hungry.'

My left-hand neighbour was a poet, and he chimed in laconically, 'Five.'

In effect, it proved that there was not one of us who had not slept in that Hotel of the Beautiful Star which is always open to everybody. We had all been frequent guests there, and now we were all prosperous, and had found other and more comfortable lodgings. There is a gentler brotherhood to be found among men who have put up in that great caravanserai than can be looked for elsewhere. He jests at scars that never felt a wound, and a fellow-feeling makes us wondrous kind.

There are many people still alive who remember the name of George Dawson. There used to be thousands who recognized it with veneration and affection. He was my first chief, editor of the *Birmingham Morning News*, and had been my idol for years. My red-letter nights were when he came over to my native town of West Bromwich to lecture for the Young Men's Christian Association there on Tennyson, 'Vanity Fair,' Oliver Goldsmith, and kindred themes.

Every Sunday night it was my habit to tramp with a friend of mine, dead long ago, into Birmingham to hear Dawson preach in the Church of the Saviour. The trains ran awkwardly for us, and many scores of times poor Ned and myself walked the five miles out and five miles home in rain and snow and summer weather to listen to the helpful and inspiriting words of the strongest and most helpful man I have ever known.

I am not sure at this time of day what I should think of George Dawson if he still survived ; but nothing can now diminish the affection and reverence with which I bless his memory. I had been writing prose and verse for the local journals for a year or two. I was proud and pleased beyond expression to be allowed to write the political leaders for the *Wednesbury Advertiser*. I got no pay, and I dare say the editor was as pleased to find an enthusiast who did his work for nothing as I was to be allowed to do it. In practical journalism I had had no experience whatever; but when Dawson was announced as the editor of the forthcoming *Birmingham Morning News* I wrote to him, asking to be allowed to join the staff. I had already secured a single meeting with him a year before, and he had spoken not unkindly of some juvenile verses which I had dared to submit to his judgment.

He proved to be as well acquainted with practical journalism as myself, for in answer to my application he at once offered me the post of sub-editor. Dr. Langford, who held actual command, set his veto on this rather absurd appointment, and told me that if I wished to join the journalistic guild at all I must begin at the beginning. I asked what the beginning might be, and learned that the lowest grade in journalism in the provinces is filled by the police-court reporter. The salary offered was 25s. a week. The work began at eleven o'clock in the morning and finished at about eleven o'clock at night. I have known many sleepless nights since then; but the first entirely wakeful time I had passed between the sheets was spent in the mental discussion of that offer. There was weeping and wailing and gnashing of teeth at home when I decided to accept it. The journal was very loosely conducted—a leader in the *Birmingham Daily Post* spoke of us once as the people across the street who were playing at journalism—and the junior reporter was permitted to write leaders, theatrical criticisms, and a series of articles on the works of Thomas Carlyle, then first appearing in popular form in a monthly issue.

I have always maintained, and must always continue to believe, that there is no school for a novelist which can equal that of journalism. In the police court, at inquests in the little upper rooms of tenth-rate public-houses, and in the hospitals which it was my business to visit nightly, I began to learn and understand the poor. I began on my own account to investigate their condition, and as a result of one or two articles about the Birmingham slums, was promoted at a bound from the post of police-court reporter to that of Special Correspondent. Six guineas a week, with a guinea a day for expenses, looked like an entry into Eldorado. There was a good deal of heartburning and jealousy amongst the members of the staff; but I dare say all that is forgotten long ago.

The first real chance I got was afforded me by the first election by ballot which took place in England. This was at Pontefract, where the Hon. Hugh Childers was elected in a contest against Lord Pollington. Some barrister-at-law had published a synopsis of the Ballot Act, which I bought for a shilling at New Street Station and studied all the way to Pontefract. I sent off five columns of copy by rail in time to catch the morning issue of the paper, and received the first open sign of editorial favour on my return in the form of a cheque for ten pounds over and above my charges. The money was welcome enough; but that it should come from the hands of my hero and man of men, and should be accompanied by words of unqualified approval, was, I think, more inspiriting than anything could possibly be to me now. A very little while later Dawson came to me with a new commission.

'I hate this kind of business,' he said, 'but it has to be done, and we will do it once for all.'

There was an execution to take place at Worcester. One Edward Hughes, a plasterer, I think, had murdered his wife under circumstances of extraordinary provocation. The woman had left him once with a paramour, and when she was deserted he had taken her back again. She left him a second time and was again deserted, and again he condoned her offence. She left him a third time, and he went to look for her. She was living in clover, and she jeered when he begged her to return. It was set forth in evidence that he had told her that he would see her once more. He walked home—a distance of three or four miles—borrowed a razor, returned to the house in which the woman was living, asked for an interview outside in the darkness, and there almost severed her head from her body. He surrendered himself immediately to the police, was tried for his life, and sentenced to be hanged.

Rightly or wrongly, the man's story inspired me with a dreadful sympathy. I cannot help thinking to this day that the tragedy of that man's life went unappreciated, and that his long-suffering devotion and the passion of jealousy which at length overcame him might have furnished Shakspeare himself with a theme as terrible as he found in 'Othello.' Anyway, the man was to be hanged and I was deputed to attend the execution.

At that time I had never been a witness at a death scene. I have seen thousands hurried out of life since then; and though even now I should find an execution ugly and repellant, I recall with some astonishment the agony of horror which this commission cost me. I had an introduction to the sub-sheriff and another to the governor of the gaol; and I presented these at the gaol itself on a night of rainy misery which was in complete accord with my own feelings. I went hoping with all my heart that the permission to attend the awful ceremony of the next morning would be refused. It was accorded, and I left the gaol in a sick whirl of pity and horror.

I shall remember whilst I remember anything my last look at the gloomy building from the fields which lie between it and the town. The flying afterguard of the late storm was hurrying across the sky, the fields were sodden, and rainpools lay here and there reflecting the dull steely hue of the heavens. A single light burned red and baleful in one window, and right over the black bulk of the gaol one star beamed. It seemed to me like a promise of mercy beyond, and I went back to my hotel filled with thoughts which will hardly bear translation.

Next day I had a first lesson in one or two things. I saw death for the first time; for the first time in my life I saw a human creature in the extremity of fear, and I had my first lesson in human stupidity. I have told the story of this execution in another place and have no mind to repeat it here. But I shall never forget the spidery black-painted galleries and staircases and the white-washed walls of the corridor. I shall never forget the living man who stood trembling and almost unconscious in the very gulf of cowardice and horror. I shall never forget the face of the wretched young chaplain who, like myself, found himself face to face with his first encounter with sudden death, and who, poor soul, had over-primed himself with stimulant. I shall never forget, either, that ghoul of a Calcraft, with his disreputable grey hair, his disreputable undertaker's suit of black, and a million dirty pin-pricks which marked every pore of the skin of his face. Calcraft took the business business-like, and pinioned his man in the cell (with a terror-stricken half-dozen of us looking on) as calmly to all appearance as if he had been a tailor fitting on a coat.

The chaplain read the Burial Service, or such portion of it as is reserved for these occasions, in a thick and indistinct voice. A bell clanged every half-minute or thereabouts, and it seemed to me as if it had always been ringing and would always ring. I have the dimmest notion—indeed, to speak the truth, I have no idea at all—as to how the procession formed and how we found ourselves at the foot of the gallows. The doomed man gabbled a prayer under his breath at galloping speed, the words tumbling one over the other. 'Lord Jesus have mercy upon me and receive my spirit.' The hapless chaplain read the service. Calcraft bustled ahead. The bell boomed. Hughes came to the foot of the gallows, and I counted mechanically nineteen black steps, fresh-tarred and sticky. 'I can't get up,' said the murderer. A genial warder clapped him on the shoulder, for all the world as if there had been no mischief in the business. Judging by look and accent, the one man might have invited the other to mount the stairs of a restaurant. 'You'll get up right enough,' said the warder. He got up, and they hanged him.

Where everything was strange and dreamlike, the oddest thing of all was to see Calcraft take the pinioned fin-like hand of the prisoner and shake it when he had drawn the white cap over the face and arranged the rope. He came creaking in new boots down the sticky steps of the gallows, pulled a rope to free a support which ran on a single wheel in an iron groove, and the man was dead in a second. The white cap fitted close to his face, and the thin white linen took a momentary stain of purple, as if a bag of blackberries had been bruised and had suddenly exuded the juice of the fruit. It sagged away a moment later and assumed its natural hue.

I learned from the evening paper and from the journals of next morning that the prisoner met his fate with equanimity. I think that in that report I bottomed the depths of human stupidity, if such a thing is possible. I had never seen a man afraid before; and, when I found time to think about it, I prayed that I might never see that shameful and awful sight again.

II

I WROTE three small-type columns—three columns of leaded minion—about that execution, describing everything I had seen with a studied minuteness. Dawson was nervous about the whole affair, and, whilst the copy was yet in the hands of the printer, asked two or three times what had been done with the theme. He was kept at bay by the sub-editor, who scented a sensation, and was afraid that the editor-in-chief might cut the copy to pieces. Dawson was purposely kept waiting for proofs so long that at last he went home without seeing them; and he often spoke to me afterwards of the rage and anguish he felt when he opened the paper at his breakfast-table and found that great mass of space devoted to the report of an execution. He began, so he told me, by reading the last paragraph first; then he read the paragraph preceding it; and next, beginning resolutely at the beginning, found himself compelled to read the whole ghastly narrative clean through. The machine was at work all day to supply the local demand for this particular horror, and Mr. George Augustus Sala wrote specially to ask who was the author of the narrative. I began to think my fortune made.

The journalist is like the doctor, his services are in requisition mainly in times of trouble. The Black Country which lies north of Birmingham is full of disaster, and the special correspondent has a big field there. Quite early in my career I was sent out to Pelsall Hall, near Walsall, where a mine had been flooded and two-and-thirty men were known to be in the workings. I was born and bred in the mining district, and was familiar with the heroism of the miners. They are not all heroes, and even those who are are not always heroic. But use breeds a curious indifference to danger.

I remember once paying a visit to the Tump Pit at or near Rowley Regis at a time when the men were taking their midday meal. There was a sort of Hall of Eblis there, a roof thirty feet high or thereabouts, and the men sat in a darkness dimly revealed by the light of one or two tallow candles. Down in the midst of them fell a portion of the rocky roof—enough to have filled a wheelbarrow, and enough certainly to have put out the vital spark of any man on whom it might have fallen. One coal-grimed man, at whose feet the mass had fallen, looked up placidly and said, ' That stuck up till it couldn't stick no longer;' and that was all that was said about the matter. I suppose there was a tacit recognition of the fact that the same thing might happen in any part of the mine at any moment, and that it was useless to attempt to run away from it. A passive scorn of danger is an essential element in the miner's life, and when need arises he shows an active scorn of it which is finer than anything I have ever seen in battle.

The Pelsall Hall Colliery disaster was the hinge on which the door of my fate was hung. I wrote an unspeakably bad novel which had that disaster for its central incident, and it was published from Saturday to Saturday in the *Morning News*, to the great detriment of that journal; and so long as the story ran, angry subscribers wrote to the editor to vilify it and its author. There was some very good work in it none the less;

and an eminent critic told me that, though it was capital flesh and blood, it had no bones. It resulted years afterwards in 'Joseph's Coat,' which is, if I may say so, less inchoate and formless than its dead and buried original.

But it was not that exasperating novel which made the Pelsall Hall disaster memorable in my personal history. I made an acquaintance there—an acquaintance curiously begun—which did much for me. I met there the king of all special correspondents, and had an immediate shindy with him. There was only one decent room to be found by way of lodging in the village, and this was in the cottage of one Bailey, a working engineer. Mr. Bailey, without his wife's knowledge, had let that room to me for a week at a rent of one sovereign, and Mrs. Bailey, without her husband's knowledge, had let the room at a similar rent to the great Special. Box and Cox encountered, each determined on his rights and each resolute to oust the other.

I was leaving the cottage at about seven in the morning, when I met a man in a flannel shirt with no collar attached to it, a three days' beard, a suit of homespun, and heavy ankle jack-boots much bemired with the clay of the rain-sodden fields. He smoked a short clay pipe and looked like anything but what he was—the comet of the newspaper firmament.

'What are you doing here?' he asked. The manner was aggressive and dictatorial, and I resented it.

'Is that your business?' I retorted.

'Who are you?' he asked. I told him that I was the representative of the *Birmingham Morning News*, but questioned his right to the information.

'Look here, young man,' he said; 'there's only one spare room in that cottage, and it belongs to me. I've rented it from the woman of the house for a pound a week.'

'And I have rented it,' I answered, 'from the woman's husband for a pound a week.'

'Well,' said the great man with much composure, 'if I find you there I shall chuck you out of window.'

I told him that that was a game which two might play at; at which he burst into a great laugh and clapped me on the shoulder. We agreed to take bed and sofa on alternate nights, and there the matter ended; but I found out my rival's name, and would have been willing, in the enthusiasm of my hero-worship, to resign anything to him. Anything, that is to say, but my own ambitions as a journalist and the interests of the *Morning News*.

Here was a chance indeed. Here was a foeman worthy of any man's steel. To beat Archibald Forbes would be, as it seemed then, to crown oneself with everlasting glory, and I was not altogether without hope of doing it. For one thing, I was native to the country-side. I spoke the dialect, and that was a great matter. Forbes was incomprehensible to half the men, and three-fourths of what they said was incomprehensible to him. There was to be a descent and an attempt at rescue on the midnight of the third day after the breaking in of the waters, and I had secured permission to accompany the party.

I hired a horse at a livery-stable at Walsall, and had him kept in readiness in the back yard of a beerhouse. My giant enemy, after maintaining a strict watch on matters for eight-and-forty hours at a stretch, had gone to bed at last, convinced that nothing could be done. It was a dreadful night, and not an easy matter for one unaccustomed to the place to find his way to the pit's mouth. The iron cages of fire that burned there in the windy rain and the dark impeded rather than helped the stranger on his way towards them. The feet of thousands of people, who had visited the spot since the news of the accident was made known, had worn away the last blade of grass from the slippery fields and had left a very Slough of Despond behind them. I was down half a dozen times, and when I reached the hovel where the rescue-party had gathered I was as much like a mud statue as a man. Everything was in readiness, and the descent was made at once.

We were under the command of Mr. Walter Ness, a valiant Scotchman, who afterwards became the manager of her Majesty's mines in Warora, Central India. Five or six of us huddled together on the 'skip,' the word was given, and we shot down into the black shaft, which seemed in the light of the lamps we carried as if its wet and shining walls of brick rushed upwards whilst we kept stationary. In a while we stopped, with a black pool of water three or four fathoms below us.

'This 'll be the place,' said one of the men, and tapped the wall with a pick.

'Yes,' said Mr. Ness, 'that will be about the place; try it.'

The man lay down upon his stomach upon the floor of the skip and worked away a single brick, which fell with a splash into the pool below. Then out came another and another, until there was a hole there big enough for a man to crawl through. We had struck upon an old disused airway which led into the inner workings of the mine. One by one we snaked our way from the skip into the hole; and, whatever the miners thought about it, it was rather a scarey business for me. We all got over safely enough and began a journey on all fours through mud and slush five or six inches deep. Here and there the airway was lofty enough to allow us to walk with bent heads and rounded shoulders. Sometimes it was so low that we had to go snakewise. There was one place where the floor and roof of the passage had sunk so that we actually had to dive for it. This seemed a little comfortless at the time, but it saved our lives afterwards. After a toilsome scramble we came upon the stables, and found there the first dead body.

It was that of a lad named Edward Colman, who had met his death in a curious and dreadful manner. He was sitting on a rocky bench, and at his feet lay a rough hunch of bread and meat and a clasp-knife. He had heard evidently the cry of alarm, had sprung to his feet, and had struck the top of his head with fatal force against a projecting lance of rock immediately above him. There had been a speedy end to his troubles, poor fellow, and he sat there stiff and cold and pallid, staring before him like a figure in an exhibition of waxworks.

The waters barred our further descent into the mine, but there was a belief that by breaking through the earthy wall of the stable a continuation of the old airway would be found. The experiment was tried with an alarming result. No sooner was the breach made than a slow stream of choke-damp flowed into the chamber, and the lights began to go out one by one. We scrambled back at once for our lives, and once past the pool were safe; the water effectually blocked the passage of the poisonous gas. I got but one whiff of it; but it gave me a painful sensation at the bridge of the nose which lasted acutely for some days. In all, our expedition had not lasted an hour; but it had proved to demonstration the impossibility of saving a single life.

I was dressed and mounted in another quarter of an hour and scouring hard through the dark and the rain in the direction of Birmingham. When I arrived there the country edition of the *News* was already on the machine and the compositors were leaving work. Word was given at once, however, the whole contingent detained, and I sat down to write an account of the night's adventure— the printer's devil coming for the copy sheet by sheet as it was written, and each folio being scissored into half a dozen pieces so that as many men as possible might work on it at once. I slept a few hours, and then rode back to Pelsall with a copy of the paper in my pocket. Forbes packed up his belongings an hour later and left the scene.

I had an idea that I had made an enemy, and that Forbes would never forgive me for beating him. I did not know my man, however; for it was he who took me by the hand in London a year afterwards and secured for me the first regular engagements I ever held there. He introduced me to Edmund Yates, who found me a place on the original staff of the *World*, and to J. R. Robinson, manager of the *Daily News*, who gave me a seat in the gallery of the House of Commons and a chance to show what I was good for as a descriptive writer. Forbes did more than this; but the matter I have in mind is private and confidential. I have no right to speak of it here, except to say that it was an act of large-hearted generosity performed in a fashion altogether characteristic of the man, and that I shall never cease to be affectionately grateful for it.

There were two instances of escape at the Pelsall Hall disaster which seem worth recording. Every mine has what is known as an 'upcast shaft'—a perpendicular tunnel which runs side by side with the working shaft, and is connected with it at the foot by an airway which serves to ventilate the workings. When the first rush of water, breaking in from some old deserted working, came tearing down, a man and a boy were standing at the bottom of the downcast. They were carried on the crest of the wave clean through the airway, borne some distance upwards in the upcast, and were there floated on to the floor of a skip, where they were found insensible, but living, some hours later. No other creature was brought to bank alive.

One special correspondent turned up at Pelsall on a Sunday, just as the pumping apparatus, which had broken down, was on the point of being repaired, and when everybody concerned was working for the bare life. It had not then been finally established that hope was over, and everybody was inspired with an almost superhuman vigour. The correspondent, who was a mighty person in his own esteem, sent his card to the manager, who sent him back a sufficiently courteous message, saying how busy he was and asking to be excused for an hour or two.

'Take back that card,' said the special (I was a witness of the scene), 'say that I represent' (he named one of the most influential of the London dailies), 'and that I insist upon an interview.'

This time a sufficiently discourteous message came back; and the mighty personage, after loafing about for an hour or two, retired and wrote an article in which he described the people of the Black Country as savages, and revived a foolish old libel or two which at one time had currency concerning them. The old nonsense about the champagne was there, for one thing. I know the Black Country miners pretty well—I ought to do so, at least, for I was born in the thick of them and watched their ways from childhood to manhood—and I never knew a working miner who had so much as heard of champagne. Now and then a prosperous 'butty' (*Anglicè*, chartermaster) may have tried a bottle; but the working collier's beverage is 'pit beer.' The popular recipe for this drink is to 'chuck three grains of malt into the cut, and drink as much as ye like of it.'

I remember the story of one wine party which met at the Scott's Arms at Barr. I dare say Mr. Henry Irving knows the house, for he is President of the Literary Society there. The tale was told me by the landlord. Three chartermasters sat at a table in the bar, and old Pountney overheard their whispered talk.

'Didst iver drink port, Jim?'

'No; what is it?'

'Why, port—port wine; it's a stuff as the gentlefolks is fond on.'

'I reckon it'll be main expensive, then.'

'Oh, we can stand it amongst the three on us. Got any port wine, landlord?'

'Yes, some of the finest in the county.'

'What's it run to?'

'Seven-and-six a bottle.'

'They figured it out,' the landlord told me, 'with a bit of a stump of an ode pencil on the top o' the table, and when they'd made up their minds as siven and sixpence was half a crown apiece amongst the three on 'em they ordered a bottle. I sent my man down the cellar for it, and I went out to look at my pigs. When I come back again there they was sittin' wry-mouthed an' looking at one another, wi' some muddy-lookin' stuff in the glasses afore 'em. "Gentlemen," I says, "ye don't seem to like your liquor." "Like it!" says one on 'em; "if this is the stuff the gentlefolks drinkin', the gentlefolks is welcome to it for we." I turns to my man, and "Bill," says I, "where did ye get this bottle o' port from?" "Why," he says, "I got it from the fust bin on the left-hand side." "Why, you cussid ode idiot," I says, "you've browt 'em mushroom ketchup!"'

III

It was on May 25, 1865, that I enlisted in her Majesty's Fourth Royal Irish Dragoon Guards. I was just past my eighteenth birthday, and, for reasons not worth specifying nowadays, the world had come to an end. Civil life afforded no appropriate means of exit from this mortal stage, and I was in a condition (theoretically) to march with pleasure against a savage foe. I was ignorant of these little matters, and was not aware of the fact that the Fourth Royal Irish was mainly a stay-at-home regiment.

My ardour for the military life was cooled pretty early. I dare say that things have mended somewhat in the last seven-and-twenty years; but my experience was in the main a record of petty tyrannies and oppressions, at the memory of some of which my blood boils even unto this day. There is a comic side to everything, however, and I can laugh over a good many of my own experiences. I had a dinner engagement that day with a friend in the Haymarket, and finding myself a little too early for it, I stood to watch the fountains playing in Trafalgar Square. My mind was in a state of moody grandeur, which is both comic and affecting to recall at this distance of time. I was quite a misunderstood young person, and was determined to be revenged for it, on all and sundry, myself included. The blue-coated brass-buttoned old spider who came to weave his web around me had no need to be elaborate. I closed with him at once, and he led me with a stealthy seeming of indifference into a back yard, where he put the statutory questions and handed over the statutory shilling.

I had supposed that I should at once enter upon my military career, but, to my surprise, I was ordered to report myself at the depôt at St. George's Barracks on the following day at noon. Failing this, I was instructed that I should be held a rogue and vagabond, and should be liable to a period of imprisonment. I went on to dinner, and bore myself there with a mysterious gloom, which, as I learned long afterwards, gave rise to a good deal of conjecture. Next day I was sworn in in a frowsy back room behind the Westminster Police Court, and learned that I was now formally bound to the service of her Majesty for a term of twelve years, my sole hope of escape being the payment of a sum of thirty pounds as purchase-money.

My military ardour had been a little cooled already at the medical examination, where, to my horrible embarrassment, I was made to strip stark naked, and was inspected by an elderly gentleman in a *pince-nez*, with half a dozen uninterested people looking on, amongst them two or three louts in fustian who were awaiting their turn. I was put into a variety of postures, all of which I felt to be ridiculous and humiliating; and when this ordeal was over there came the swearing-in and a visit to the depôt canteen, where I received payment of a sum of seven and sixpence and was introduced to some of the raw material of the fighting forces of the nation.

I may say quite frankly that I did not like the raw material. The young men who composed it were without exception vulgar and loutish. Their language was absolutely unreportable, and they were all more or less flushed with beer. I had been almost a total abstainer all my life, and though I drank a little of it out of complaisance I thought the canteen tack the nastiest stuff I had ever tasted. The depôt barrack-room in which the recruits slept until the time of their deportation echoed morning, noon, and night with unmeaning ribaldries and obscenities, and was stale with the smoke of bad tobacco and the fumes of that most indifferent beer. I learned that I was bound for Ireland, and that the head-quarters of my regiment were at Cahir. One respectable old depôt sergeant took some interest in my quiet and isolation.

'You'll be out of this lot soon,' he said, 'and you'll never see anything like it again. These chaps'll learn manners when they join the colours; and you're lucky in the regiment you're going to—there's no smarter in the service.'

I have made one or two uncomfortable journeys in my time, but I can recall nothing quite so comfortless as the march with that ragged and disreputable contingent along Piccadilly, across Hyde Park, down the Edgware Road, and so on to Paddington Station. It was all very well for the sore and rebellious heart to be singing inwardly, ' Yes, let me like a soldier fall ; ' but this was a sordid beginning for military glory, and I would sooner have been shot outright than I would have encountered anybody I knew on that journey. I reached the station unobserved, so far as I know, and was glad to hide myself in a third-class carriage, into which the sergeant in charge of the party beckoned me. He was very kind and friendly indeed, advising me in a score of ways suggested by his own experience, and talking constantly with his hand upon my shoulder. I had begun to think him quite a genuine good fellow, and my heart was warming to him, when he let the cat out of the bag.

I was handsomely attired, and the morning suit I was wearing was barely a week old. He was good enough to offer me ten shillings and a rig-out for a scarecrow in exchange for it. I declined the friendly offer, and the sergeant cooled. He condescended to accept a drink at Didcot Junction; indeed, he did me the honour to ask for it; but when it was consumed he ordered me into a carriage already fully occupied by half a score of my fellow recruits, and in their society I finished the journey to Bristol.

We put up at the Gloucester Barracks, which, as I understood, had once been an hotel, and the escort sergeant, who had turned spiteful, set me to work to carry coal upstairs.

This was my first experience of fatigue duty, and I was kept at it till I was very fatigued indeed, and my smart summer trousers and spick-and-span shirt-cuffs were a little damaged. This duty over, I met the escort sergeant no more, but was transferred to the care of a quaint old boy who made an astonishing display of learning. He had four or five Latin proverbs at his command. He knew the Greek alphabet, had picked up a bit of Hindostani on Indian service, and a little bit of French and Turkish in the Crimea. All these he aired upon me in a very natural manner, and I was much impressed with his erudition, until a grinning depôt man got me into a corner and told me that 'the sergeant had shown me the whole bag o' thricks at wonst.' He paid every well-dressed recruit that compliment, it seemed; and the depôt man warned me that he too would make a bid for my clothes, and would offer me a scarecrow rig-out in return.

'If ye'll take my tip,' said the depôt man, 'ye'll say neither yes nor no till ye get to barracks. Kape the ould blagyard hangin' on and off till ye get inside the gates, and then tell him to go to blazes. If ye loike to work him properly, ye can kape him as smooth as soft soap all the way. If ye say no too early he'll be on t'ye like a ton o' pig-iron. It's the truth I'm tellin' ye,' he added, 'as sure as God made little apples.'

He thought his advice was worth a drink. I thought so too, and he got it.

We steamed away next day in the *Apollo*, bound for Cork. We had a rough passage, and the depôt sergeant took me into his private cabin and cheered me with a glass of whisky, the first I had ever tasted. He began, when he had thus softened my heart, to try the bargain about the suit of clothes, and produced a set of garments the like of which I do not think I ever saw.

'You'll not be allowed to keep these,' he explained, fingering me all over to test the quality of the cloth I wore. 'You'll be in regimentals in a day or two, and it'll make no difference to you.'

One of the officers of the vessel looked in whilst this business was going on and broke in gruffly, 'You join your regiment looking like a gentleman, young man. Your officers won't think any the worse of you for going in decent. Damn it all, sergeant, what d'ye want to spoil the lad's prospects for?'

So a second time the suit was saved; but it went a week later to an old soldier who was leaving the regiment and whom it fitted to a hair. He was to leave a certain portion of his kit behind for me, which, as he assured me, would be of the utmost use; but he sold such articles as belonged to him to the men in his own barrack-room that evening, and decamped without seeing me again.

The stormy passage ended delightfully amidst the quiet beauties and serene shelter of the Cove of Cork. I have seen a great many of the world's show-places since 1865, and I dare say that my inexperience counted for much; but I cannot recall any natural spectacle which afforded me a more genuine delight. It was the morning of the 30th of May. The sun was just rising, and the roofs and spires of the city were outlined against a lucent belt of sky. Spike Island lay green and smiling in the middle of the cove; and on either side, on the emerald slopes, white villas were dotted here and there. The whole scene looked very sweet and pure and homelike, and there were certain thoughts in my own mind which made the view memorable.

We were all bundled up to the Cat's Hill Barracks, and there held over Sunday. My companions melted away unregarded, and I travelled down to Cahir under the charge of a decent old fellow who did not try to buy my clothes, but spent a good deal of time in exhorting me to write to my friends and beg their pardon for having made a fool of myself.

'Ye'll be doing it late,' he said, ' and ye may as well be doing it soon.'

I was quite lonely and sore enough to have taken the advice, and military glory looked a long way off; but a silly pride withheld me, and I pretended to feel well satisfied with my prospects and surroundings.

When I came to understand things a

little I could see that the regiment was in a splendid state of discipline and efficiency. It had not been so a few years before, when the Lieutenant Robinson episode at Birmingham had brought the command of Colonel Bentinck into grave disrepute. Lieutenant-Colonel Shute, on whom the actual charge of the regiment devolved, set to work to bring cosmos out of chaos; and did it, though it took him a day or two of very uphill work. I know more of what a regiment should be than I did then, and I do not ask a firmer or a more judicious discipline. The men were enthusiastically loyal to their colonel, and believed in him as if he had been a sort of deity. I am persuaded that they would have gone anywhere and have done anything for him. There is nothing the British soldier respects like justice, and he likes it none the less if it is a little stern. We all had a holy dread of the colonel, though he was not a bit more of a martinet than any good officer should be; and his wife, who had a habit of giving autographed Prayer Books to the men, was regarded with a genuine affection.

I found the men, in the main, very good fellows indeed. Of course there were all sorts among them. Many were well bred and well educated, and one or two might have been met without surprise in almost any society. Some, again, were thorough-going blackguards, and others, who were among the most popular and the best soldiers, were incurably rackety and undisciplined. One man, who had thrice won his stripes as full corporal, was for the third time broken and reduced to the ranks during my first month of service. He would keep away from drink for two or three years at a time, and then in a night would undo all the results of hard work and self-denial. Take the men in the main, and it would be difficult to find a better lot; but the petty officers seemed to make it the business of their lives to put the heaviest of burdens on the shoulders of any promising recruit. They were none of them very well educated, and I suppose that it was only natural that they should fear the advancement of a youngster better tutored than themselves, and should do their best to keep him down. One only found this disposition amongst the younger non-coms.—men who had not held their places long enough to grow used to the dignity of rank.

There is, or was in my time, a soldiers' proverb, 'As nasty as a new-made corporal.' With one exception the sergeant-majors were good fellows and popular with their men. I shall not give the name of the exception, for he may be still alive; but he was commonly known as 'The Pig,' and he deserved his title. There was no meanness and no denial of military etiquette of which he would not be guilty to get a man into trouble. One badgered private assaulted him violently with a pitchfork, and suffered two years' imprisonment for that misdemeanour. 'The Pig' was quite uncured by this experience; and one night, prowling round the barrack-rooms after 'lights out' to see if he could find an after-dark smoker, he was assailed with a tremendous shower of highlows from every quarter of the room. The cavalry highlow, well aimed and low, as Count Billy Considine said about the decanter, may be made a very effective missile, and its powers of offence are not diminished by the fact that it pretty often carries a spur in the heel of it. This event was spoken of with bated breath about the regiment for a day or two, but nothing came of it. 'The Pig' was by no means sure of his popularity with his superiors; and there is an admirable and most trustworthy military tradition to the effect that no good officer is ever assaulted by his men.

IV

THE Fourth Royal Irish prided themselves particularly, and not without reason, on the smart and soldierlike aspect of the regiment. Recruits were looked on with a jealous eye, and a gawky or loutish fellow was received with open disfavour. While we were at Cahir a couple of young fishermen from the North of Ireland joined. They came in sea-boots, pilot-cloth trousers, and knitted jerseys; and they were for a while objects of derision. I dare say one story is remembered in the regiment still. They were sent into the riding-school before they had had time to get their regimentals. It is no easy business for any unaccustomed person to mount a saddled horse without the aid of stirrups, and the young sailors in their huge sea-boots were at a double disadvantage.

'I can't get aboard this here craft nohow, Captain,' said one of them to old Barron, the riding drill. I shall never forget his expression of contempt and scorn as he saw the young men ignominiously hoisted into the saddle. At the first order to trot the fishermen hung on desperately to saddle and headstall.

'Jack,' said Barron, wrinkling his red nose in disdain, 'look out, or you'll be overboard!'

'Not me,' says Jack; 'not so long as the bloomin' riggin' holds.'

The sea-going brethren turned out very smart soldiers later on; but within a month of their arrival there came about the most hopeless specimen I can remember to have seen. His name was Sullivan, though he pronounced it Soolikan, and he was an embodiment of every awkwardness and stupidity. He was a shambling, flat-footed, weak-kneed, round-shouldered youth, and the Fourth asked with amazement how on earth the doctors had been induced to pass him. So far as I remember, he never learned anything. The various drills laboured at him like galley-slaves, but never succeeded in teaching him the difference between 'port arms' and 'carry arms.' When he had been diligently instructed in the sword exercise, he asked the sergeant what was the use of it all. 'While I was going through that,' says he, 'some bloody-minded Russian 'd be choppin' me head off.' It was his idea that a soldier was supposed to go through the sword exercise in face of the enemy; and the notion that it was simply intended to give dexterity in the use of the weapon never occurred to him.

There was never anything in the world more hopeless than the attempt to teach Soolikan to ride. Of course he was never trusted in the *manège*; but he tumbled about on the tan of the riding-school in an astonishing manner, breaking no bones and incurring, somehow or other, no sort of damage. Every morning the recruits led their horses into the school and mounted there, and every morning old Barron addressed his *bête noire* in the same words, 'Pick a soft place, Sullivan.' It was all very well so long as the ride circled at a walk at the lower end of the school. But then came the order, 'Go large!' and shortly afterwards the long drawling command, 'Tr-r-o-o-o-t!'

The horses, which were old stagers and

knew the words of command far better than their riders, started at the beginning of the note; and before the call had well ended the brisk impressive 'Halt!' would snap across it like a pistol-shot. 'Pick up Sullivan, somebody!' The luckless man, after more than three months' lessons, came to me one morning in triumph and told me with a broad grin, 'I didn't fall off the day.' He was recognised from the first as incorrigible, and when he had spent but four months in the regiment he disappeared. It was darkly whispered in the barrack-rooms that he had been told to go, and that he had been bribed with a ten-pound note to desert the regiment. I dare not mention names; but I think I could lay my hand on the gallant officer who went to this expense for the credit of the corps.

I suppose the School Boards have done

much within the last score of years to minimise the mass of popular ignorance; but in '65 one found here and there an amazing corner of mental darkness amongst the rank-and-file of a dandy regiment like the Fourth. There was a great hulking fellow named Gardiner, who was boasting one day that he could carry twice his own weight. He was told that he could not so much as lift his own, and was persuaded into a two-handled hamper, in which he made herculean efforts to lift himself. There was another man who received with perfect gravity the chaffing statement of a comrade, to the effect that he had shot a wood-pigeon at the North Pole, and that the bird had fallen on the needle on the top of the Pole, and had frozen so hard that it was impossible to remove it.

'Ye know the song,' said the humourist, " True as the needle to the pole." There's no gettin' the needle out of the Pole, and now there's no gettin' the pigeon off the needle.'

The man for whose benefit the narrative was told smoked his pipe stolidly, and answered, 'Begorra, but it must be cold up there!'

Some of the men had odd ideas about the uses to which learning should be put. One came to me on a Sunday afternoon bearing a Bible, with a request that I would find for him and read to him all the indelicate passages. I met this proposal with so loud a negative, and heaped such invective on the head of its author, that the corporal of the room, who was smoking a tranquil pipe outside, came in to find out what was the matter, and, being satisfied, fell to beating the man about the head with a boot. From the person thus chastised I heard no more of the matter; but I learned enough from others to know that my refusal had not helped to make me popular. There was a tacit sense to the effect that I was not a friendly fellow—that I was not willing to share the results of my reading with the less favoured.

At this distance of time I can write dispassionately; but for many years I had recollections of petty tyrannies which made my blood boil. There was a lanky youth, four or five months older in the regiment than myself, who was related to one of the sergeant-majors, and who was, of course, booked by his relative for promotion. It was never, so far as I can learn, a part of army etiquette, but it was a common practice at that time, to steal the belongings of a new arrival, and in that way to eke out a deficiency in the kit of the plunderer. My valise had not been served out to me a week before it was denuded of one-half its contents, and I was reduced to a draft of one penny a day for pocket-money until such time as the depredations were made good. The sergeant-major's nephew was found in the act of pipe-claying a pair of gauntlet gloves which bore my number, and the immediate consequence of this was a stand-up fight in the riding-school in the presence of some fifty or sixty of the men and two or three officers who looked on from the gallery. I came out more than conqueror and recovered the stolen property; but the lanky young man was made lance-corporal next week, and it became part of his duty to instruct me in military exercises in which I was far more proficient than himself. It became a regular habit of his to keep me at work while the rest of the squad stood at ease, and he had a vocabulary which, though limited and unoriginal, was as offensive as can easily be conceived.

He applied to me at last so vile an epithet that, in the heat of the moment, I forgot that I had a sabre in my hand, and, hitting out straight from the shoulder, I landed him on the mouth with the guard of the weapon. This, of course, was flat mutiny, and before I knew where I was I was seized from behind, the sabre whirled in the air, and I was lying all abroad with a sprained wrist. Then I was solemnly marched to the guard-room, and there taken in charge to await an interview with the colonel in the morning.

One of the men on guard had borrowed from the regimental library a copy of Charles Reade's 'It is Never too Late to Mend,' and I read that masterpiece all the afternoon and as long into the night as the waning light would allow. The guard-room bed, with its sloping board and wooden pillow, made no very luxurious sleeping-place, and I was up at daylight to finish the most absorbing and enchanting story I had ever, until then, encountered. The book retains a great portion of its old charm and power until this day for me, but at that time it shut out everything ; and though, for aught I knew to the contrary, I might be sentenced to be flogged or shot, I resigned myself to the spell of the story as completely as if the future had been altogether clear. The colonel was rather dreadful when the time came, and I remember one axiom which I got from him in the first three minutes of our interview.

'Well, what have you to say for yourself ? '

'The fact is, sir,' I answered, ' this man has been most abominably insolent.'

'Nonsense,' said the colonel ; 'a private can be insolent to his superior ; a superior cannot be insolent to a private.'

I doubt whether the gallant colonel would have felt inclined to sustain that thesis in the House of Commons, of which assembly he afterwards became a popular and honoured member; but I dare say it did very well as an orderly-room apothegm. It had to come out, however, that the newly-made lance-corporal and I had had a fight a week or so before the date of his promotion, and that I had come out uppermost. I spoke of the corporal's language, but declined to repeat it. One of the squad, who was called in evidence, was less particular, and the colonel, in effect, read the young non-com. a dreadful lesson and committed me to cells for ten days, giving orders that I was not to be disgraced—by which was meant that I was not to receive the prison crop which is made to mark the ordinary turbulent soldier. From that time care was taken that the lanky youth no longer had me in charge; but we used to scowl at each other when we passed, and for a year or two after my return to civil life I cherished a warm hope that I might meet him and repeat in his society the exercise I had so sweetly relished in the riding-school.

After this episode the crowd was down upon me. It was felt that I had triumphed, and it was felt that no recruit had a right to triumph over any officer, however young or however lowly placed. Even a lance-corporal must be respected, or it was clear that the service was going to the devil. A brace of sergeants, with whom I had been none too much of a favourite already, laid themselves out to get me into trouble, and the plan they adopted was delightfully simple and easy. It is the rule on retiring from the *manège* to make the grooming of one's horse the first duty, though an old soldier will take the precaution on wet or muddy days to run an oily rag rapidly over the burnished portions of the horse's fittings in the first instance. This is a labour-saving practice and is almost universally followed. But I saw one of my enemies with a sidelong eye upon me, and tackled my horse at once. In two minutes his confederate was round.

'What the ———' (any competent person who knows barrack life can fill in the blank) 'do you mean by letting your bridoon and stirrup-irons lie rusting here? Put 'em in oil at once.'

Number Two, having delivered this order, went away, clothed with curses as with a garment, and back came Number One.

'Now, what the ———' (break to be filled as before, for these people have no sense of style or invention) 'do you mean by leaving your horse to stand and shiver in that beastly lather? A nice bargain the Queen made when she gave a bob for you!'

This form of insult is traditional, but at first hearing it has power to gall. The discovery that it is no more than a formula takes off its edge. Back to the horse, to be again assailed by Number Two for not having obeyed the order about the bridoon and stirrup-irons. Back to them, and then the last scene in the comedy, in which, under a charge of neglecting to groom my horse in spite of repeated warnings, I was marched straight to the orderly-room, there to appear before the colonel.

I boiled over in his presence and denounced the little conspiracy. The colonel was something of a martinet, but he was justice incarnate. Witnesses were called from the stable; my story was made good; and as I stood in the ante-room adjusting my forage-cap I heard the beginning of a tongue-walking which those non-commissioned officers were not likely to forget.

'If you dare to bully my recruits again,' said the colonel, 'I'll break the pair of you. I won't have my recruits bullied.'

I smiled at this; but I was not allowed to enjoy a further triumph. The orderly sergeant wrathfully ordered me away, and I went back to my duty. From that hour any question of comfort in the regiment was, of course, over, and it would take a volume to tell the history of the shifts and dodges which made life unbearable; though, of course, that history would be worth neither the writing nor the reading. Most of the officers were invariably kind and considerate; but there was one whom I never forgave until I learned, years afterwards, that he was dead. It was my habit to think and believe of him that he was the stupidest person that ever sat upon the magisterial bench in any capacity, civil or military. A wider experience of the world has modified that opinion, but he deserves a place in this record for all that.

He was a pale-faced man, with a slight lisp; and the men despised him because he had not the nerve even to handle them on church parade without priming himself beforehand. I had been vaccinated by virtue of a general order, and in a while my arm became swollen and very painful. I stuck to duty as long as I could, and at last presented myself on hospital parade to ask to be excused. The doctor, for some reason, was absent, and, failing his order, I was compelled to join the ride in the *manège*. It was a beastly morning, and the field was a mere bog. We were splashed to the very buttons of our forage-caps, and the horses were loaded with mud to the flaps of the saddles. I was tired and faint enough before the ride was over, but my poor beast had to be groomed on the return to stables, and I must needs set to work upon him. It was all no good. I might as well have tried to carry him as to groom him, and I represented my case to a non-commissioned officer, who straightway ran me in. I passed the night in the guard-room, chilled and wet, and now and then light-headed. Had I been at head-quarters the colonel would undoubtedly have sent me to the infirmary, which was the proper place for me. The lisping captain sent me to the cells.

'Ma-an,' he said, in a drawl which half the regiment used to loathe and imitate, 'what have you to tha-ay?'

I explained my case, and whilst I did so he read something which lay on the table before him. When I had done he said, with his finicking lisp, 'Seven days' cells, hard labour.' The old regimental sergeant happened to be there, and for an instant arrested judgment.

'I beg your pardon, sir, the man is really unfit to perform hard labour.'

'Then,' said the Solon, 'in that case let him have forty-eight hours' solitary confinement.'

I ventured as respectfully as I could to protest. I represented that it was hardly just to punish a man for not performing a heavy physical task whilst admitting in the very terms of the sentence that he was unfit to do it. The answer was, 'Right about face, march!' I went to cells. I had my hair cut, and I spent thirty-six delirious hours alone. At the end of that time my condition was reported and I was removed; but from that hour I was sullen and rebellious, and whatever spirit of order and discipline might have lived in me until then vanished completely.

Only four years ago, on a very memorable occasion in my life, I sat side by side with one of my old officers. He assured me, with every appearance of gravity, that if I had stayed much longer I should have disintegrated the regiment. I was sure, on the other hand, that the regiment would have disintegrated me; and though I was smart enough and willing enough to have made a good soldier at the beginning, I was too angry at stupidity and injustice to care to please anybody any longer. I knew one man who, having been gently nurtured, found himself suddenly thrown upon his own resources. He enlisted with a full determination to rise. When I last heard of him, years ago, he held brevet rank in another regiment; but I know what slights he endured, to what numberless insults he submitted, and how harsh and cruel the pathway to success was made for him at the beginning. They tell me things are better now, and I hope with all my heart they may be. As I knew the ranks they were made well-nigh intolerable for any well-educated youngster who showed a disposition to get on.

V

THOUSANDS of people remember the excitement created five or six years ago by the story of the Missing Journalist. Scores still cherish the memory of poor MacNeill and think of him as amongst the cheeriest, friendliest, and most helpful of men. He was a delightful fellow and a good fellow; but he had a certain boisterous exaggeration of manner which sometimes made his friends laugh at him. So far as I know, he neither had nor deserved an enemy through all his effusive, genial, and blameless life.

He burst into the Savage Club one day when I happened to be there alone. He was unusually radiant and assured, and ' At last, at last,' he said, ' I've got my foot on the neck of this big London!' The triumphant phrase set me thinking at the moment, and has often recalled to me since, the time when this big London had its foot on me: a thing of the two which I am afraid is the much more likely to happen in the experience of any young aspirant to literary honours when he has neither friends nor money to back him, and no reputation to begin with.

I came to London just after the opening of the Parliamentary session of 1872, at a time when every nook and corner of the journalistic work-room was filled, and when the doors were besieged, as they always are at such a season, by scores of outsiders eager for a turn at the good things going. I forget now precisely how it came about, but I went to live at a frowsy caravanserai in Bouverie Street, an astonishingly dirty and disreputable hotel called the 'Sussex.' It is down now, and its site is occupied by the extended offices of the *Daily News*; but in its day it was the home of as much shabby gentility as could be found under any one roof in London. Beds were to be had there at threepence and sixpence. I remember no arrangement for meals, and certainly never troubled the establishment in that way myself. The linen had a look of having been washed in pea-soup and dried in a chimney, and the whole aspect of the house and its *clientèle* was wo-begone and neglected to the last extreme. Paper and pen and ink are cheap enough, and I used to sit all day long in my bedroom, fireless in the winter weather, wrapped up in an ulster and with a counterpane about my knees, writing for bare life. I wrote verses grave and gay, special articles, leading articles, and leaderettes. These were delivered at all manner of likely and unlikely places, and came back again, like the curses and the chickens and the bad penny in the proverbs.

I lived for weeks on hard-rinded rolls and thick chocolate, procured at an Italian restaurant on the opposite side of Fleet Street, and found myself admirably healthy on that simple diet. I wrote now and then to friends in the country, disguising my estate, and telling them what I was working at without hinting what became of the work when it was finished. One of my correspondents remonstrated with me for taking up my quarters in a hotel in that part of London, and advised me to try cheaper lodgings. Until I had something regular to rely upon, I was told, it was absurd to launch into an extravagance of that sort. I have often had to think how many hundreds of men, better equipped for the intellectual arena than I was, as plucky, as determined, and as full of hope, have gone down in the lonely and bitter sea of poverty in which I floated in those days. My breakfast expenditure of threepence, with a halfpenny to the waiter, secured me a look at the daily papers, and every morning I went back to that beastly bedroom to write at my dressing-table in denunciation of the Ministry, or to hold up to public contumely some unpaid justice of the peace who had given a hungry labourer six months for stealing twopennyworth of turnips. I redressed countless wrongs on paper in that draughty garret; but nothing came of it. There is no use in being too minute in narrating the history of that time. It was bad enough to begin with, and grew at last to be about as bad as it could be. That obliging uncle, who becomes your aunt when you cross the Channel, was useful for a time. But at last there was nothing more for him to take or for me to offer, and I was alone in London with a vengeance.

Thousands of well-to-do people endure privation and discomfort every year for the pure pleasure of it. In my campaigning days I lived on black bread and onions and dirty water for seven weeks, and topped up that agreeable record with four days' absolute starvation. But I had a pocketful of money, though there was nothing to be bought with it, and I had staunch comrades, and we were marching on with the certainty of plenty before us. It was all endured easily enough, and now and then there were outbursts of rollicking jocundity in spite of it. The mere physical suffering of privation is not a thousandth part of its pain. The sense of loneliness, of defeat, of unmerited neglect;

the blind rebellion against the inequality with which the world's chances are distributed; the impotent sense of power which finds no outlet—these are the things which make poverty bitter. But there was nothing else for it, and I took up *la vie en plein air.*

My favourite chamber in the Hotel of the Beautiful Star during the hours of darkness was the Thames Embankment. I have passed many years in London since then, and must have heard the boom of Big Ben and the monotonous musical chime which precedes it many thousands of times. They have rarely greeted a conscious ear without bringing back a memory of the stealing river (all dull shine and deep shadow), the lights on the spanning bridges, the dim murmur of distant traffic, the shot-tower glooming up against the sky, the bude-light flaring from the tower of the Palace of Parliament, the sordid homeless folks huddled together on the benches, the solemn tramp of the peeler, and the flash of the bullseye light that awoke the chilled and stiffened sleepers. There is a certain odour of Thames Embankment which I should recognise anywhere. I have encountered it often, and it brings back the scene as suddenly and as vividly as the chimes themselves.

There is plenty of elbow-room in the Hôtel de la Belle Etoile, and there is water enough; but in other respects the provision it offers is scanty and comfortless. I spent four days and nights in it, and was on the borders of despair, when what looked like a mere chance saved me. Suppose I had not walked down Fleet Street; suppose I had not stopped to look at the little cork balls in Lipscombe's window, so mournfully emblematic of my own condition; suppose that the unsuspected good-hearted friend had not come by and clapped me on the shoulder, what would have happened? *Quien sabe?* These are the narrow chances of life which give one pause sometimes. He came, however, the unsuspected helpful friend.

It was John Lovel, then manager of the Press Association. I have since had reason to believe that he deliberately deceived me from the first moment of our encounter, and that later in the day he was guilty of a plagiarism. If deceit were always as kindly and guileless, lying would grow to be the chief of human virtues; and if plagiarism always covered a jest so generous, the plagiarist would be amongst the most popular men alive.

Was I busy? he asked. Was I too busy to undertake for him a very pressing piece of work he had on hand? I made an effort not to seem quite overborne, and told him that I was entirely at his service. He said (I suppose it was the first thing he could think of) that to-morrow was the anniversary of the birthday of Christopher Columbus. He wanted an article about that event for a country paper and had no time to write it. He wanted no dates, no historic facts, but simply 'a good, rattling, tarry-breeches, sea-salt column.' The pay was a couple of guineas; and if I could so far oblige him as to let him have the article that morning, he could make it money down.

I wrote the article in the reporters' room at the P.A. and sent it in to the chief. In return I received a pill-box, on the top of which was written, 'The prescription to be taken immediately.' I found within the pill-box two sovereigns and two shillings wrapped in cotton-wool, and I went my way to a square meal with the first money I had ever earned in London. I found out afterwards that the date was nowhere near that of Christopher Columbus's birthday; and, so far as I know, the article I had written was never used. I was telling the story years afterwards, and somebody informed me that the prescription on top of the pill-box was Thackeray's. I was quite content to discover that, and I don't think poor Lovel would have minded it either. He paid the debt of nature some time ago, and when he left this world had the memory of more than one good deed to sweeten his parting moments.

I went back to that gruesome hostelry and wrote an article on 'Impecunious Life in London.' It appeared in the *Gentleman's Magazine*, then published by Messrs. Grant & Co. and under the editorship of my old friend Richard Gowing. The article was

not far from being autobiographical. I think
—but I am not quite sure—that I got sixteen
guineas for it. I know that it set me on my
feet, and that since then any acquaintance I
may have had with the Thames Embankment
has been purely voluntary.

Poverty makes a man acquainted with
strange bedfellows; and I made one or two
queer acquaintances on the Thames Embankment and acquired a taste for vagabondising
about among the poor which lasted a year or
two and has proved to be of no small service
since. Slumming had not become a fashion
at that time of day; but I have never aimed
at being in the fashion, and I did a good deal
of it. Through Archibald Forbes's kind
offices, I found an introduction to the *World*
journal, and, at Edmund Yates's instigation,
wrote a series of articles therein under the
title of 'Our Civilisation,' picking up all the

quaint and picturesque odds and ends of humanity I could find in London.

I met many people whom it was very difficult to describe and impossible to caricature. Amongst them was a street artist who lived in Gee's Court, off Oxford Street— a worthless, drunken, and pretentious scoundrel, who seriously believed himself to be the most neglected man of genius in London. I employed him to repeat what he called his *chief de hover* on cardboard, and paid him half a crown for it. He called this work 'The Guard Ship Attacked.' It represented a Dead Sea of Reckitt's Blue with two impossible ships wedged tightly into it, each broadside on to the spectator. From the port-holes of each issued little streaks of vermilion, and puffs of smoke like pills. The artist gloated over this work, and was ready to resent criticism of it like another Pietro Vanucci. He told me he was unappreciated; that he was a man of the supremest talent, and was kept out of the great theatres, where he could have shone as a scene-painter, by nothing but the pettiest and shabbiest jealousies. I don't know where he had picked up the phrase, but he had something to say about the dissipation of the grey matter of the brain, and he returned to it fondly as long as I would allow him to talk to me. His artistic labours and his art invention were dissipating the grey matter of *his* brain. All he asked for was a fair field and no favour. If I would give him three pound ten he could buy an easel, a canvas, and a set of painting tools, and would at once proceed to show the Royal Academy what was what.

I was well to do by this time, but yet not quite wealthy enough to venture on such an experiment. The most amusing thing this vagabond said was when he found in my room the painting materials and sketches of an artistic friend of mine with whom I was chumming at the time. His nose wrinkled with an infinite disdain as he turned the sketches over, and he said, with a delightful air of patronage, 'I see, I see. A brother of the brush.' He brought with him on his journey from Gee's Court to the north of London an incredible ghoul of a man, a creature whose face was muffled in a huge beard alive with vermin. He, it seemed, was another neglected man of genius; but I declined to be introduced to him. I looked up the artist's address, however, and got to know his neighbourhood pretty well. Boulter's Rents, in my first novel, 'A Life's Atonement,' were drawn from Gee's Court.

I thought the picture rather like at the time, within limits; but I never had the heart—or the stomach—to be a realist. Feebly as I dared to paint it, I had to re-form it in fancy before the book was finished. The original horror stands there, pretty much unreformed; though I dare say its walls get a coat or two more whitewash than they did when I was intimate with them.

I have kept for this place in a rambling record a story which might have been told in my last paper. When I left the barracks of Ballincollig and said good-bye to her Majesty's service, I had an encounter with one of my non-commissioned enemies. I had my leave of absence in my pocket, and my discharge was to follow me by post. I was in civilian dress and was smoking a cigar at the barrack gates. My enemy saluted before he had had time to recognise me, and then, seeing to whom he had done this homage, stood abashed at himself for a minute and then exploded. He could think of nothing better to say than to order me to put out my cigar. I refused to obey, for I was yards beyond the magazine limit, within which it was, of course, forbidden to smoke, and I gave that sergeant a piece of my mind. One is a good deal more vehement at nineteen than one grows to be when creeping on towards the fifties, and I made my sergeant a dreadful promise. I told him that he had acted like an unmitigated brute to me, and I undertook, if ever I should meet him in civil life, to inflict upon him a chastisement which should repay us both amply. I never met him again for thirteen years, and I was slumming when I ran against him. He was acting as commissionaire at a big manufacturing place in the East End, and when I accosted him he had no idea of my identity. I wore a beard and had taken to wearing spectacles, and, if ever I had looked warlike, had lost that aspect long ago. I asked him if he were Sergeant ——. He admitted that at once. He had served in the Fourth Royal Irish?

'Seventeen years, sir; but I don't remember you.'

He had been quartered at Cahir, I reminded him, in the year '65, and in '66 at Ballincollig. He admitted that quite willingly and seemed interested. Did he remember a recruit who was nicknamed 'Oxford?' He thought he remembered that recruit, and paled visibly. He was not the stalwart fellow he had been, but looked bowed down as if by a premature old age. I asked him why he had left his regiment.

'Hernia, sir; hernia and pulmonary consumption.'

I had promised this man a hiding thirteen years ago, and thirteen years ago I am persuaded he had richly merited it, and am quite sure it would have done him good. It is very likely that at that time I might have been unable to give it him; but now, between a florid manhood on my side and hernia and pulmonary consumption on his, the task should have been easy. But the events of '65-'66 looked a long way off in '78; and somehow it seemed hardly worth while to reveal one's identity. So the sergeant got half a crown and was left with a bit of a puzzle to occupy his leisure moments.

VI

I HAVE seen a good deal of the working of the English Poor-law, and have learned to have some decisive opinions about it. It has always seemed to me, since I had any acquaintance with it at all, that it might have been constructed on purpose to restrict the free action of honest labour and to set a premium on idle vagabondage. I determined, fourteen or fifteen years ago, to put the system to a test in my own person, and for my own sake to start with the odds in favour of the institution. My belief was, and is, that no law-abiding man could travel in search of work through England under the provisions of the Poor-law without danger to health and even life, whilst any worthless and shiftless idler can by its provisions eke out a tolerably comfortable subsistence.

I got me a shabby suit of clothes, sent a portmanteau to the place where I intended to end my journey, and, posting a ten-pound note in advance, carried a money order for that sum in the lining of my hat. Thus provisioned, and with a shilling in my pocket, I started to walk towards the money. I was David Vane, compositor, and it was my object to see if David, with the best will in the world, could live under Poor-law provisions without bringing himself into the mesh of the policeman's net. I gave him seven weeks of it, and walked over half the south, midland, and western counties; giving him an occasional rest in a cheap lodging-house when workhouse fare had come to be too much for him.

When I came to a town where my money lay at a post-office, I drew a shilling or two and sent the bulk on further; but during the whole seven weeks I only trespassed on my hoard to the extent of fifty shillings. Without that hoard, or without a breach of the law, my imaginary compositor would surely have died. I see now and again in the newspapers a sporadic correspondence about the treatment of men on tramp, about the food supplied them, the hours of their imprisonment, and the amount of labour they are compelled to perform. I notice that chairmen of boards of guardians are quite satisfied with the existing condition of things. I encounter, in the newspapers, gentlemen who have tasted workhouse skilly and soup, and who like it, and consider it well made and nourishing. I meet others who account the sleeping accommodation good, the bread excellent, and the labour demanded no more than reasonably adequate. I should ask nothing better than to see these easily contented gentlemen each enjoying a seventh part of my personal experience.

I may say at once that my notes of this journey were destroyed years ago, and that I cannot tell with absolute certainty in what places certain things happened. My experiences were challenged at the time, and the challengers got little good by their denial of my statements. I had hoped that my Quixotic enterprise might have some good result, but the absurd old system has undergone no alteration.

It was in a green lane in Oxfordshire that I came across my first travelling companion. He was a man of about sixty, a decent-looking old fellow, and, as I found out when I got into talk with him, by trade a tailor. He had stopped to bathe his feet in a little brook spanned by a single arch of mossy brickwork, and whilst he cooled his feet in the stream he rubbed his cotton socks with a bit of yellow soap the size of half a crown. He was civil and ready to talk; but he was very downhearted. He showed me his fingers, the tips of which were raw and smeared with tar.

'That's this morning's work,' he said. He named the workhouse he had stayed in. 'That's put me off earning a living for a good week to come. A man can't sew whilst his fingers is in this state. Stone breaking's bad enough; but when it comes to oakum-picking it's all up with work for one while. There was another chap there last night,' he went on, 'as I should take to be worse off than me. He's a watchmaker. Dressed very nice and tidy he was, and got a job to go to in the town this morning. He begged hard to be let off, and offered to pay for his night's lodgings if they'd let him. They kep' him to it, hows'ever, and he did his work. *I* wouldn't ha' done it,' he concluded. 'I'd ha' gone afore the Bench first; though that ain't mostly any good in these 'ere country places.'

This disclosure interested me, for I myself belonged provisionally to one of the light-fingered professions. It would be about as easy for a compositor to earn a living fresh from oakum-picking as for a tailor or a watch-maker; and I determined, if that task were set before me, to plead my trade and see what came of it. I had no longer to wait than next morning; but when the work was given out it looked to my ignorant eye so inconsiderable that I forbore to make any complaint about it. A piece of old tarred rope, six or seven inches long and an inch and a half in diameter, had to be picked into fine oakum between seven o'clock in the morning and eleven. The business looked anything but formidable, and I began upon it with a light heart.

The accustomed men began by hammering the ends of their strands upon the stone floor, and I followed their example, and, having secured a hold for the finger-tips, went ahead with the work. I may say that until a man of delicate fingers has tried this occupation he can have no idea of the long-drawn and exasperating misery of it. It is no use to be impatient, for in attempting to go too fast you succeed only in skinning your thumb and fingers. The only chance is patience, and that is not an easy thing. The old stagers, who had had years of it, got along quite comfortably, and were thankful that they were not stone-breaking. The new men swore and grumbled and flayed their fingers. The result of my own experience was that David Vane, compositor, was put beyond the chance of earning a living at his legitimate trade for a good fortnight. The accommodation paid for by the labour consisted, all told, in one hunk of dry bread—weight, I should say, about four ounces; one pint of stirabout made of Indian meal and flavoured with soot; and a particularly dirty and uninviting bed. Having bestowed these benefactions on the harmless workman, the British Poor-law in return insists that he shall become a hopeless pauper by stealing from him his handicraft.

I tried stone-breaking pretty often later in the course of my tramp, and found it a much less painful occupation. The handling of cricket-bat and sculls hardens the palm of the hand whilst it leaves the tips of the fingers unprotected. But though at the time of my excursion I was fresh from life on the river, it took me some time to get inured to this new occupation, and stone-breaking alone would, of course, unfit for his work any man who needed lightness and steadiness of hand. Work and accommodation varied very widely. In one or two places we got good bread at night, good broth in the morning, and a bed to sleep in which, as I suppose, the average tramp would find almost luxurious. The bed-clothes were coarse, as they had a perfect right to be, but they were clean ; and the food, though scanty and of the plainest, was wholesome and nourishing. In one place, I remember, the bread actually stank, and the hungriest of the hungry crowd left it uneaten. The broth served out next morning was nothing more or less than the water in which bacon had been boiled. The beds were kennels. A long wooden bench was divided into compartments by upright boards; a quantity of dirty straw which might, by the look of it, have served already in a stable was spread in each recess, and was covered with foul sacks which bore the name of a local miller. Several of these sacks, cut open and stitched together, served for a counterpane.

'I'd 'eard about this place,' said my neighbour when the able-bodied pauper who superintended us had trooped us into this abominable chamber, 'and I'd a dam good mind to smash a lamp or summat and get run in instead o' comin' here. If I'd ha' knowed the truth about it, I'd ha' done it.'

This was the worst, and by far the worst, of the places I encountered. Indeed, I met nothing else comparable to it. I made a trifling error in my description of it at the time. By a slip of the pen I represented the shed in which the casual paupers were accommodated as being a lean-to against the body of the workhouse, whereas it was in fact a lean-to against the outer wall of the workhouse grounds. This was enough in the minds of the guardians to justify them in denouncing me, through their chairman, as a liar, and was held to be triumphant proof that I had never been there, though I proved 'David Vane, compositor,' upon their books and upon those of the two neighbouring workhouses.

In some country places we went straight to the relieving officer, who gave us our tickets for the night. In other places of more considerable population we were allowed to lounge about the outside of the police station until the hour appointed for distribution. Once inside the workhouse, we were prisoners until at least eleven o'clock next morning whether the tale of stones were broken or no, or the strands of rope were or were not reduced to oakum. In default, men were occasionally detained to be taken before the Bench ; but what became of them I never had an opportunity of learning apart from the experiences of my travelling companions, who estimated the punishment at seven or fourteen days. A good many of these had gaol experiences, and I am forced to admit that the decent folk on tramp were few in number. But the occasional honest mechanic or skilled workman in search of employment was hard bestead.

I met two journeymen printers, one of whom, having threepence for a bed outside the workhouse, was able to find employment in the town of Gloucester ; whilst the other, being unable to get away from durance before eleven, was left out in the cold. I met other men who, in order to escape this absurd imprisonment, slept in the fields, and so risked liberty on the other side rather than miss the early labour market ; for to sleep in the fields is a misdemeanour punishable at law : though why it should be so, if nothing else be provable against a man, Heaven only knows. In the language of the road, to sleep in the open is to 'skipper' and to sleep in the workhouse is to go 'on the spike.' It was a common question in fine weather, 'Skipper or spike to-night?' The habitual loafer invariably chose the spike. The man who had business and wanted to get along elected to skipper, though he lost two meals thereby.

The law, which ruins the hands of the skilled workman, and detains skilled and unskilled alike until the labour market is closed to them, supplies a dietary which would kill anybody but a professional fasting-man in a month, and keeps a keen eye on mendicancy. It is like the sun, with a difference: it looks alike on the just and the unjust. The mischief is, it is made for the comfort of the worthless and is the plague of the deserving. There are easy-going boards of guardians, easy-going workhouse masters and labour masters, who do not insist upon the tale of work which is demanded by others. The old stagers know the easy places and give them a natural preference.

The one place of terror on the line I took was Gloucester. The guardians of the Gloucester Union had made up their minds to put down the casual pauper, and, as the means readiest to hand, they determined to make the work too hard for him. I was so persistently warned against Gloucester that I went there to see for myself what it was like. The house itself was orderly and clean, and the discipline as complete as in a gaol. The only thing which distinguished it from other places of its kind was the severity of the labour imposed.

The limits of labour are fixed by law. There is such and such a weight of oakum to be picked, or such a weight of stone to be broken ; but the good guardians of Gloucester, without in the least infringing the provisions of the Poor Law Board, made the work twice as severe as it was in other houses than their own. Before every casual pauper was placed the regulation quantity of stone—it was the hardest I tackled on my pilgrimage—and beyond the morning's stint was set a screen through which every atom of the stone had to be passed before the job was finished and the wanderer was allowed out upon his way again. It was no business of mine to be refractory, and I hammered away with such zeal as I could command; but it took me six hours to get through the tale of work. When I had earned my own discharge I left a handful of unfortunates behind me who had theirs yet to finish. They were all unaccustomed and inexperienced, or they would not have been at Gloucester. Whether that charming western city keeps up its reputation until now I do not know; but the guardians found their system succeed so well that they have probably adhered to it. I had forgotten to mention one fact which is common to all workhouses. The casual tramp breakfasts when he has done his work, but not before.

Discerning private critics of my novels have noticed how much capital I have made of this odd adventure. In 'A Life's Atonement' Frank Fairholt goes on tramp, seeking to efface himself amidst the offscourings of the poor after an accidental deed of homicide. In 'Joseph's Coat' Young George goes on tramp, slinking from casual ward to casual ward until he meets Ethel Donne at Wreathdale. In 'Val Strange' Hiram Search on tramp opens the story; and it was by way of spike and skipper that John Jones, of Seven Dials, brought fortune to his sweetheart in 'Skeleton Keys.' I fully admit the impeachment, and, indeed, I am not indisposed to brag about it. Perhaps few writers of fiction have gone as close to nature for their facts.

I met more queer people and found more queer adventures on that tramp than I have ever been able to find a literary use for. One amazing vagabond with a moustache announced himself to me, when I had found a way into his confidence, as a professional deserter. He had enlisted in every militia regiment in the country and in half the regiments of the line. When he had secured the first instalment of his bounty he made a bolt of it, and, by way of securing safety, took immediate refuge in the next military depôt. I understood that he had pledged himself to serve her Majesty for a period of something like a thousand years. Wherever I had the chance to test him I found him a most enterprising liar, and I dare say he exaggerated a little here. I asked him what trade he followed or professed between whiles. The rascal grinned with a delightful cunning and said he was a hand comb-maker.

'The trade's dead,' he told me; 'machinery's knocked the bottom out of it. There's only one shop in England where they makes combs by 'and nowadays, and you can bet as *I* steers clear o' *that*. It's a lovely lay to go on, matey. "The trade's ruined," you says, "by machinery," you says. "I was brought up to it for a livin'," says you, "an' it's the only thing," you says, "as I've got to yearn my daily bread by the sweat of my brow by," you says. Lord! I've had as much as ninepence in a day out o' that yarn on the very road as we're a travellin' now.'

I had a qualm of conscience; but his artless tale was told, as it were, under the seal of confession, and I never betrayed him.

VII

It was at least as agreeable to starve on the non-proceeds of landscape painting as on those of journalism, and when nothing in the way of meat and drink was to be got out of either, it was only a choice as to the form of euthanasia. I guessed I could make no money out of painting; but I knew by practical experience that there was nothing to be made by journalism.

I was daubing in a friend's chambers when the angel of opportunity came. He appeared in the form of an American gentleman with a fur collar and an astonishing Massachusetts accent. War had been actually declared between Russia and Turkey a week or two before. The Russians were already at Giurgevo, building a bridge of boats with intent to cross the Danube, and the Turks were gathered in force at Rustchuk and Schumla. So much I knew from the newspapers, but no further intelligence of the opening campaign had reached me.

My visitor's card announced him as Colonel——, and he bore a letter of introduction from the representative of a leading New York journal. He was himself in London as the representative of a newspaper published in Chicago, and in the course of a five minutes' conversation he told me that he was in search of a young, healthy, and enterprising journalist who was willing to risk his life for the honour of his craft, and a rather considerable sum per column for copy delivered at the office of the newspaper of which he made himself the flying herald. The only engagement I had in the world was to breakfast with a man on Sunday morning, and that I waived instantly. An immediate 40*l.* was put into my hands; an arrangement was made that on calling at the American Embassy at Vienna I should receive more, and that at the bank at Constantinople I should find a sum of two hundred sterling on arrival. With this understanding I started for the seat of war at seven o'clock on the following morning, and in due course found myself at Vienna. There I tried, in pursuance of instructions, for an interview with the Turkish Ambassador, who steadfastly declined to see me. I made certain necessary preparations, and called at the bank half a dozen times over. There was no hint or sign of my Chicago friend; and possibly if I had been more experienced than I was I might have at once taken warning and returned home. As things were at the time no such idea entered my head; and when, after a delay of two days, half the promised money reached me, I took ticket gladly for Trieste, and embarked on a Messageries Maritimes boat for Constantinople.

It was the twelfth of May of that year when we set sail down the Adriatic, and I had never seen anything so heavenly beautiful as the coast and sea. We were five days on our journey; and now, when I have travelled the wide world over, have seen most of its show places, and have made myself familiar with exotic beauties of the landscape and seascape sort, I can recall nothing like that five days' dream of heaven. Perhaps the fact that I was going to look at war for the first time, and had some premonition of its horrors, made the placid loveliness of the Mediterranean more charming and exquisite by a kind of foreseen contrast. But I do not remember to have beheld (and I do not think I shall fail to remember it all till the day I die) anything so beautiful as the far-off islands that lifted their purple heads as we steamed through the Piræus, and the long-drawn wonderful panoramic splendours of the Mediterranean sunsets. I have travelled in many ships since then, and have never missed the inevitable fool. There is always a fool aboard ship; and I remember one day when we were within sight of Corfu that the fool who was our local property for the moment touched me on the shoulder as I hung over the bows, and pointed to the island.

'They say that's land,' said he, ' but you'd think it was a sweetmeat. Looks good to eat, doesn't it? It's like them biled violet things in sugar that they sell in Paris.'

I was all on fire to see the interior of my first Eastern city, and when I saw the domes and minarets of Constantinople actually before me, the traveller's instinct was quickened to a passion. We got in at sundown, and behind the picturesque roofs of the town lay an amber and crimson mystery of light, which was half-obscured by the smoke and steam of a score or two of vessels. The whole scene looked like a smeared landscape from the hand of Turner. He, at least, would have seen to it that the colour was clear; but Nature is very often behind the artist, and the effect was grossly muddy and untransparent.

In common with the rest of the world I had heard of baksheesh, but until then I never understood its magic power. A huge functionary took charge of my trunk and portmanteau, and impounded them so decisively in the name of the law that I had made up my mind to see neither of them any more. The captain of the boat whispered in my ear that a mejidieh would do it. I tried a French five-franc piece, which proved instantly efficacious; and a minute or two later I was on shore at Galata, astride a donkey whose tail was industriously twisted round by his driver, and who was followed by an unequally laden brother ass, who bore my portmanteau on one flank and my trunk upon another.

We scrambled up the stony road towards the main street of Pera. The city had looked like a Turneresque dream from the outside, but known from within it was the home of ugliness, and of stinks innumerable. The yellow dogs tripped the feet as often as the abominable pavement, and seemed as immovable and as much a part of the road itself. Now and again in the side streets a whole horde howled like a phalanx of advancing wolves; but they were outside the parish of the brutes who encumbered the roadway I had to travel, and though the noise of war was near, the canine regiment not actually called to fight rested immobile, its members suffering themselves to be kicked by foot passengers, trodden on by cattle, and rolled over by wheels with an astonishing stolidity.

We reached the hotel in time for an admirable dinner—the precursor of many admirable meals, whose only fault was that they were built too much on one pattern. We were served, as I recall too well, with tomato soup, red mullet, quail, tomato farcie, and cutlet. Next morning at breakfast came red mullet, quail, and tomato farcie. At luncheon came red mullet, quail, tomato farcie, and cutlet. At dinner came tomato soup, red mullet, tomato farcie, quail, and cutlet. It was a charming menu—for once: but when we had gone on with it for a week my travelling companions and myself grew a little weary of it, and would fain have found a change. Poor Campbell—Schipka Campbell we called him afterwards—had arrived with an earlier boatload of adventurers and was staying at the Hôtel de Misserie. Captain Tiburce Morrisot, of the Troisième Chasseurs, stayed at the Byzance; and we three made a party together to dine at Valori's and to escape the eternal red mullet, tomato farcie, and quail.

We found there an astonishing German waiter who seemed, more or less, to speak every language under heaven. There were in the café Greeks, Italians, Spaniards, Turks, Bulgars, Germans, Frenchmen, and

Englishmen, and people, for aught I know, of half a dozen other nationalities; and the head waiter addressed each and all of these in turn in any language which might be addressed to him. One of us asked him with how many tongues he was familiar, and he answered, with an apologetic aspect, 'Onily twelf.' What could we have for dinner? 'Fery good dinner, gentlemen. There is red mullet, there is tomato farcie, there is qvail.' We elected finally to dine on something which was announced as roast beef and looked suspiciously like horse. Anything was better than that eternal round of delicacies which had grown to be so tiresome.

The city was in a state of siege, and every ramble along the street was productive of interest and amusement—sometimes of a rather striking sort. I had only been there some three or four days when, in the course of a morning stroll, I found myself in front of the Wallach Serai. The footpaths were lined pretty thickly with loungers who had stood to watch the march-past of a regiment of Zeibecks. The bare-legged ruffians, with their amazing beehive hats and their swagging belly-bands crammed with the antique weapons with which their ancestors had stormed Genoa, straggled past in any kind of order they chose to adopt and made their way towards the Sweet Waters of Europe, by whose shores they were destined to encamp. When they were all gone and the stagnant tide of passage was revived there came by an old Hoja, a holy man, dressed in green robe and caftan and wearing yellow slippers—self-proclaimed as one who had made the pilgrimage to Mecca. He was followed by a very small donkey laden with panniers. By my side on the footwalk stood a Circassian who had been flourishing in the air, whilst the troops went by, a formidable-looking yataghan, and had been cheering in some language of which I did not understand a syllable.

This man was now standing, with an admiring crowd about him, licking the back of his wrist and shaving off the hair that grew there by way of showing the edge and temper of his weapon. It must have been set as finely as a razor, and, like a razor, it was broad-backed and finely bevelled. Just as the old Hoja went by, and the placid little donkey followed at his heels, the Circassian stepped into the horse-road, gave the weapon a braggadocio swing, and at a single blow divided the head of the poor little ass from the body as cleanly as any dandy swordsman of the Guards will sever a hanging sheep. The head fell plump; but for a second or two the body stood, spouting a vivid streak of scarlet from the neck, and then toppled over. The old green-clad Hoja turned at the noise made by the crowd, saw the blood-stained sword waving behind him, understood at a glance what had happened, and shuffled on as fast as his yellow pantoufles would carry him.

VIII

IT is probable that there never was in the history of the world a city so crammed with every sample of the tribes of rascaldom as Constantinople at this epoch. I saw, from the carriage gateway at the Hôtel de Byzance, three coffee-coloured scoundrels pause at the place of custom held by an itinerant money-changer. The man sat with his little glazed box of Turkish and foreign coins before him on the pavement, his whole financial stock-in-trade amounting to perhaps twenty or thirty pounds. One of the passing rascals offered for his inspection a diminutive gold coin, and the grey-bearded, venerable-looking money-merchant, having examined it, opened his case and took out a handful of coins to give change for it. The glass lid was no sooner lifted, than each one of the trio dipped in a coffee-coloured paw and took out a handful of money. The man who had shown the small gold coin pouched it again and walked on. The poor old money-changer rose to his feet and made a motion as if he would follow; but one of the ruffians half drew the sword which hung at his side, and turned upon him with a sudden snarl. The old man sat down to his loss, and made no further attempt to recover his stolen belongings.

Wandering up and down the city I was witness to a score of acts of equal lawlessness, and in point of fact the whole place was a prey to a restless terror. Between the city and the Sweet Waters of Europe there was an encampment of perhaps the most remarkable and varied assortment of blackguards that ever got together in the history of civilised warfare. Until they were known, the curious citizens used to ride out to look at them and wander about the camp; but one or two days' experience cured the people of Constantinople of this habit. A Greek lady and her daughter were hideously done to death by the encamped ruffians, and the coachman who strove to rescue them had his throat cut. Two or three events of this kind set the Christian part of Constantinople in a panic, and no white man ventured abroad after nightfall without carrying arms.

With all this the streets had never been bare. Every night the Grande Rue de Péra swarmed with passengers; the restaurants and hotels were full; and you could hear the raucous voices of the vocal failures of a dozen countries shrieking and bellowing through the open windows of the *cafés-chantants* along the street. The one place that we frequented was the Concert Flamm. It was kept by one Napoléon Flamm, who in those days was known to almost every Englishman in Constantinople. He had a little silver hell beside the concert-room, and the swindling roulette-table there was presided over by a fat oily Greek, who might from his aspect, had some friend taken the trouble to wash him, have been supposed to be a diplomat of high rank. The table, as I very well remember, had but twenty-four numbers and at either end a zero. Had the game been fair, and had all the players been skilled, the proprietor of this contrivance must have taken by mathematical law a penny out of every shilling which was laid against the bank. I make no pretence to an extraordinary credulity; but I still believe that the fat Greek had a dodge by means of which it was possible to arrest the action of the wheel at the most profitable moment.

There was a Dutchman in the silver hell one night—a gentleman who told us that he was known in South Africa as the King of Diamonds. We learned later on, from independent sources, that though he had kept the suit he had changed the card. From Kimberley to Table Bay the fame of the Knave of Diamonds had travelled, and if only one-half we heard of the man was true he had earned his title. For something like an hour and a half this gentleman and myself stood side by side at the roulette-table, and noticed unfailingly that whenever black was most heavily backed red won, and whenever the major part of the money was on red black turned up. We formed our own conclusions, and in our sober hours at least declined to play at that particular table.

There was a tremendous fight in these rooms one evening, which was begun in a comic way enough by Captain Georg von A——, of the 4th König's Dragoons—a handsome, dashing young giant of a cavalry officer, who had done excellent service against the French at Gravelotte, and who was now bent on joining that ill-fated Polish Legion which was for a while the receptacle into which was swept half the scoundreldom and half the honest adventurous spirit of young Europe.

Poor dear old Campbell, dead these many years now (he fell under Wolseley leading the black contingent on Secocoeni's Height), the young German captain, and myself, had dined together, and Von A—— had dined not wisely, but too well. He had learned a word or two of Turkish, and, supposing that the inhabitants of the Grande Rue and the frequenters of the Concert Flamm were Turks, he rose and uttered a patriotic phrase, 'Chokularishah Padishah!' which means, as I am informed on credible authority, 'May the Sultan live for ever!' All the befezzed and bearded gentry, hook-nosed, sloe-eyed and greasy of complexion, who frequented the café of Monsieur Napoléon Flamm were Greeks and Armenians, and whether the Sultan lived for ever or died next day they did not care one jot. They stared somewhat impolitely at the handsome fair-haired young German, but said nothing. He carried on his parable in Turkish: 'Muscov dormous,' and illustrated his meaning by drawing his thumb with Masonic vigour across his windpipe.

The words and the action together were meant to signify that the Russian was a hog and ought to have his throat cut. Straightway up stood a little Greek with a ' Je suis

Muscov, monsieur,' and the captain promptly knocked him down. He had not meant to do anything of the sort, but the mere windy buffet of his big hand toppled the little Levantine on to the floor. There was an immediate shindy. A coffee-cup was hurled by some indignant compatriot of the man assaulted and sent a splendid looking-glass, seven or eight feet high, to irremediable ruin.

A coffee-cup in a Constantinople café is made of porcelain as thick as a lady's little finger, and weighs something like a quarter of a pound. In less time than it takes to tell it the nationalities were mixed and sorted again. Gaul, Briton, and Teuton—there were seven of us from the north-western end of Europe—got shoulder to shoulder, and every man of us had half a score to tackle. I never saw so funny a fight in all my life, and certainly never enjoyed myself at less personal risk. The room was clear in something under five minutes, and England, France, and Germany stood triumphant. The little Levantine crowd streamed down the winding stair, and Campbell added insult to injury and injury to insult by picking up the hindmost small man and dropping him on to the heads of those who had gone before him. We all laughed heroically ; but when we got downstairs, after the outgoing crowd, the aspect of affairs was changed considerably.

I am talking of many years ago, and I am not quite certain of local names at any moment. People who know Constantinople can correct me if I mistake the name of the place; but I think it is the Rue Yildijé which stands nearly opposite the entrance to the old Café Flamm and leads, or led, to the low Greek quarter. Anyhow, there is a sloping street there which runs down by a flight of rough stone steps towards the Galata district, and from this a fierce crowd came swarming, armed with broom-handles, knives, pokers, tongs — any weapon snatched up in the vengeful tide of the moment. Poor Campbell took command of our party, formed us in line, and made us draw our revolvers. The entrance to the café was wide enough to allow us to issue shoulder to shoulder in a sort of bow. We ranged ourselves along the wall, flanked the crowd, and took up a position across the pavement. Amongst our enemies those behind cried 'Forward!' and those in front cried 'Back!' We paced backward until we reached the Byzance Hotel, some fifty or sixty yards away, and there, once within the gateway, we put up our weapons, entered the hotel, and called for drinks. In a better-regulated city we might have heard something more about it; but, as it was, nothing happened, and the Chief Constable of the Consulate—from whom, by the way, I had bought the Irish Constabulary revolver which enabled me to make my show against the crowd—joined us in the course of the evening and laughed heartily at the tale.

IX

I HAVE told how I went out as 'special correspondent' to an American paper in the Russo-Turkish war. From the hour at which we said good-bye to each other on the platform of Charing Cross railway station, some seventeen years ago, until now, I have never seen the military gentleman from Chicago at whose instance I went out to watch the events of the Russo-Turkish war. When I got home again, a month after the fall of Plevna, I made inquiries about him, and learned that he had exceeded his instructions, and that if he had followed the directions laid upon him by his proprietors he himself would have gone out to the seat of war. What object he proposed to himself in shirking that duty, and in sending out a man whose salary he could not pay, I never definitely learned.

For quite a considerable time I used to call day by day at the Ottoman Bank to ask if remittances had arrived, and so long as my funds lasted I used to bombard that recalcitrant Yankee colonel with telegrams insisting on the fulfilment of his contract. He took no notice of my messages, and in a very little while things began to look desperate. It was a great thing to be on the spot, however, and after some three weeks of fruitless anger and bitter anxiety I found casual work to do under a gentleman who had constituted himself the agent of an old-fashioned London weekly. I wrote an article for this journal, entitled 'In a State of Siege,' got money down for it, and lived carefully on it for some ten days. At the end of that time, I was strolling rather disconsolately round the Concordia Gardens at night-time, when I came upon a group of men with whom I had a nodding acquaintance. They were seated round a little table, drinking vishnap and lemonade, and chattering gaily amongst themselves. One of them called me to join the party, and another, whom I knew to be acting as agent for the *Scotsman*, was reading a newspaper. We talked indifferently for a while; and the reader, laying down his journal on the table, set his hand upon it with a solid emphasis and said, 'If I could find the man who wrote that article, I should ask him to go to the front at once.'

I glanced at the open sheet, and, lo! the article was mine. I said so, and in ten minutes I had made a bargain. I was to go up country at the earliest possible moment; and received instructions as to how to proceed in application for the necessary *teskerai*, a form of passport or safeguard without which no stranger was allowed to enter the interior. The search after that abominable *teskerai* delayed me for many days, and I danced attendance on Said Pasha (English Said as he was called) until I was weary and heartsick.

At last I determined to go without the passport, and did so; but the delay I experienced brought me into contact with as queer a body of adventurers as I ever encountered in my life. At the head of these gentlemen was a Mr. Montague Edie, or Edie Montague (for he wrote the name both ways)—a young fellow of apparently four or five and twenty, who gave himself out, I think, as a lieutenant in the English navy, and who professed to have authority from the Turkish Government to sail a war-ship under letters of marque and to harry Russian commerce in the Black Sea.

Constantinople at this time was full of hare-brained adventurers, and Mr. Montague Edie was not long in gathering about him a band of officers. The business of the expedition was supposed to be a profound secret; but it was talked about with a childish *naïveté* in all manner of public places. The chieftain laid in uniforms of his own designing, and strolled about the Grande Rue de Péra, gaudy in a Turkish military fez, white ducks and gloves, and a blue coat beplastered with gold lace. One or two of his lieutenants followed his example; and the unfortunate tailor who had provided these sartorial splendours held the Hôtel Misserie and the Hôtel Byzance in siege for days in the vain hope of extracting payment for his labours.

A droller set for the management of a

ship of war was never seen anywhere. The second lieutenant, I remember, was fresh from St. John's College, Oxford. He had left his native shores for the first time on this journey, and his whole experience of the sea had been acquired in the passage of the Channel and the voyage from Marseilles to Constantinople. Poor Schipka Campbell put him under examination one evening at a *brasserie* in the Grande Rue, and elicited the fact that he supposed port and starboard to mean the same thing, and larboard to be the antithesis of the two. I forget the first lieutenant; but a subordinate officer was a fat City clerk who had been a volunteer in some London corps, and who on the strength of his military experiences had come out with intent to seek a commission in the Polish Legion.

The peculiarity of that contingent was

that, so far as I know, not a solitary Pole ever attempted to join its ranks. The City clerk was seduced from his original purpose by the splendour of Mr. Edie's uniform. He was himself rigged out at the expense of the same unfortunate tailor who had supplied his fellow-officers; but he only wore the uniform once, having been caught and mercilessly chaffed by a contingent of British officers who were waiting for the formation of the Turkish gendarmerie under Colonel Valentine Baker. Associated with this crowd of silly and inexperienced boys was an old grey-bearded American doctor, who believed in the whole cock-and-bull story as if it had been gospel, and had undertaken to act as surgeon aboard that visionary craft. He was a delightful old fellow, and, for all his simplicity, had a vein of humour in him. Odd as it may sound, he was a man of some distinction, and had served with conspicuous honour in the Civil War. He had money of his own, and Heaven only knows how many generous things he did amongst the crowd of stranded foreigners at that time in the city.

'I don't lay out to know much,' he said to me one day; 'but I have made one discovery. Civilisation and the paper collar air *con*terminous. Turkey is a civilised country. I bought half a gross of paper collars at the Bon Marché this morning. So long as I can purchase a paper collar I know I am in a civilised country, and when I cayn't, I ain't.'

I met the doctor a day or two after the publication of this memorable discovery. He was talking with one of the officers of the expedition, and suddenly he threw the walking-stick he carried high into the air.

'That lets me out!' he said, in a very loud and decided tone; and, quitting his companion, he beckoned to me to follow him. The old gentleman's face and gesture were so urgent that I joined him at once. He told his story in a vernacular racier than I dare to copy; but it came to this. The Government had got wind of the precious scheme (to which it had, of course, never given a moment's sanction), and had come down with an intimation that the originator of it and his subordinates would do well immediately to leave the country.

The chieftain was not thus easily to be balked, however. He called a council of war, and proposed to his astonished satellites that they should steal a gun-boat and turn pirates against the Russians on their own account. This delectable scheme was instantly rejected by the gentlemen to whom it was submitted, and it was the news of it which let the doctor out. He took steamer that afternoon for Syra, and I have never since heard of him. The officers of the letter of marque surrendered their uniforms to the tailor whom they had blessed with their patronage, and the chieftain went for a day or two to the lock-up at the British Consulate.

Sir John Fawcett—Mr. Fawcett he was in those days—chose rather to laugh at the whole business than to treat it seriously, and the adventurous young gentleman was released on a promise to leave the country. I myself was offered a post of honour in this remarkable contingent. The secret at which all Constantinople had been laughing for a week was confided to me in whispers at the Concert Flamm. I think—but at this distance of time I am not quite sure—that the post offered to me was that of Captain of Marines. I don't mind confessing, in justice to my own unwisdom at that time of day, that if there had been a boat and a marine I might have thought twice before refusing the offer. As it was, of course it was simply a matter for laughter.

I hardly like to leave Constantinople without a memory of the Polish Legion. I took a journey by the Shooting Star Railway with a chance companion, to see him sworn in and receive his commission as an officer of that regiment. The place of assignation was a loft over an untenanted stable, for the time being the head-quarters of the corps. I never heard of their having any others; and I remember with unusual distinctness an interview one of the officers had with Said Pasha, who told him, with a perfect absence of reserve, that the Legion 'would be sent to the front and would be dissipated.' As a matter of fact, it never got really into form. I believe that there was never at any moment a solitary private in its ranks. So long as it lasted it consisted entirely of officers of various grades. Many of these, seeing how hopeless the whole enterprise had grown to be, abandoned it openly; others quietly slipped away without warning; and a good many willingly allowed themselves to be drafted into other regiments, where some of them did good service.

The English journalists in Turkey were divided by faction. We were mainly Philo-Turkish or Philo-Russian, according to the political colours of the journals we represented; and I know now very well that I was, for my own part, so impressed by the Bulgarian atrocities scare that I hardly knew how to look for mercy or right feeling in a Turk. The plain truth was very hard to get at, but now, through the far perspective of the years that lie between, it is easier to see with a judicial eye. If there is to be found anywhere in the world a gentler, a more hospitable, a more sober, a more chaste, truthful, and loyal creature than the citizen Turk, I confess that I should like to meet him. If there is anywhere to be found a man more devoted to duty, braver, simpler, gentler than the common soldier of the Turkish army, I would walk a long way to find him.

While the war went on, half of the men who sent the news of it out to the civilised world found the Turk *anathema maranatha*, and the other half were persuaded that the Bulgarian was a beast altogether despicable and cowardly. Since the Bulgarians have had a chance to govern themselves they have amply disproved that unfavourable theory, and 'the unspeakable Turk,' of whom we heard so much in those days, was in the main as good a sort of fellow as might be found in Europe.

The atrocities which shocked the world were, without exception, the work of the auxiliaries—the Tchircasse, the Bashi-Bazouk, the Zeibeck, the Smyrniote and Tripolite. I claim to know something of the doings of these gentry, for Mr. Francis Francis (then representing the *Times*) and myself were for six weeks the only Englishmen in what was known as the 'Roumelian atrocity district.' Day after day we lived among the Christian dead, night after night we saw the incendiary fires. From the heights of the lower Balkans—as at Sopot—we could see the horizon red. The deserted villages stank with the unburied bodies of men and animals. About them in the night-time hordes of vagabond dogs howled lugubriously in the dark.

It was wonderful and terrible to see how the old savage Eastern spirit could revive itself in these modern days—'Kill, slay! leave not one stone standing upon another.' In Kalofer, where there had been a busy and thriving population a fortnight before our arrival, there was not a creature left, and scarcely a wall on the summit of which one might not have laid one's hand. The town still sent up a melancholy smoke to heaven as we entered it late in the evening, and the last torch of war shone from a thatched roof at the uttermost limit of the place against the lowering darkness of the sky. The arabajee who drove the lumbering little vehicle in which our few belongings were stored fell upon his knees in the middle of the stony desert street, and delivered to me an impassioned address of which I could not make out one syllable. My dragoman translated for my benefit. 'Man with the two sweet eyes,' said the kneeling orator, in possible tribute to my spectacles, 'why did we enter upon this disastrous journey? Allah has forgotten us. Let us return.' We were in two minds about it already, for the place was weird to look at and the air was a slow poison; but the horses were tired, and we ourselves had had almost enough of the day's march.

Suddenly I sighted a domestic rooster, walking with a certain air of pensive reflection down the street. I rested my revolver on my left arm, took careful aim and fired. The bird towered madly, executed a wild waltz, and went round the corner. The noise of the shot disturbed some members of his harem, and a hen fluttered into the branches of a tree close by. Francis potted her, and she fell at our feet. Here, at least, was supper; but at the first corner we turned, in search of a place in which to camp for the night, we found the rest of the feathered brood feeding on the carcase of a pig which literally heaved in waves of vermin life. We were very hungry; but there was a good two to one chance that our bird had enjoyed that uninviting diet, and we threw her over the nearest wall into the cinders of a smoking cottage.

We were resigned to remain supperless, when, with a prodigious clatter on the stony street, and a wild calling of voices, came down three Turkish Cossacks, detached, to call us back, from a party of regular troops which we had passed that morning. The news they brought was, that the country was alive with every species of unconscionable blackguard known to the time and region;

and at their urgent advice we mounted our tired beasts once more, and rode until a journey of some half-dozen miles brought us to the camp. There we fed royally, and slept in safety.

X

THERE is a theory to the effect that every man or woman in the world could write at least one readable and instructive novel out of his or her own actual experience. There is a very apparent disposition to put this idea to the test of practice, though, happily, not more than half the world's population has been so far animated by it. An equally sage idea is that anybody, and everybody, can take a part upon the stage. To write a novel or to turn actor—to astonish the world with a new Waverley, Esmond, or Copperfield, or to dazzle the mimic scene with a novel Hamlet, Falstaff, Richelieu, or Othello—would seem the simplest thing in the world to the apprehension of a good many excellent people.

Charles Dickens observed a great many years ago that to 'come out' in a great part is one of the easiest things in the world; while to avoid going in again is one of the most difficult. In my time I have both come out and gone in again; and though I am not disposed to tax my modesty for defences, or to offer prophecies for the future, it is not improbable that I may repeat the experience in its completeness. I suppose that the pursuit of the successful actor is the most fascinating in the world. Here and there one learns that it has been distasteful in an individual instance; but these cases are only the exceptions which prove themselves and nothing else.

A great many people have been good enough to tell the story of my first appearance on the stage; and they have told it in ways so diverse, and yet so circumstantially, that I have been sometimes tempted to doubt the genuineness of my own recollections. Here, however, for what it is worth, is my belief about the matter.

I was in New Zealand some three years ago, when a travelling manager whom I ran across in the course of my wanderings asked me if I happened to have such a thing as a new and original drama about me. I confessed that I had a scheme for a drama in my mind (the manager confessed himself to be singularly anxious to produce it), and I undertook to finish it and to see it through rehearsal. It will be observed that none of the usual difficulties which lie in the way of the ordinary pretender to dramatic fame obstructed my progress. There was no question of suitability—no thought of excellence or the reverse. The travelling manager had anything to gain and nothing to lose by the production of a piece from my hand. It meant no more than the trouble of rehearsing; and if the thing failed, it failed and there an end; and if it succeeded, the manager stipulated for half profits wherever the piece might be produced. He has not, so far, retired from business. In the innocence of my heart I promised that the piece should be ready for rehearsal in three weeks' time, and I set to work with the greatest vigour, burying myself for the first week at Gisborne, a weird and lonely seaside town where there has as yet been no whisper of a railway, and where the steamers which ply along the coast may or may not call for the traveller, according to the weather.

If I may say so of myself without immodesty, I am a rapid and assured workman.

All my best work has been done at a tremendous pace. I turned out 'Joseph's Coat' in thirty-six sittings, a chapter at a sitting. 'Val Strange,' a work of equal length or nearly, was written in as many consecutive days. 'Aunt Rachel,' the one work of mine which may outlive me by a score of years, was written at such a pace that a copying clerk would have some ado to transcribe it in the time. Its three last chapters were written between sunset and sunrise in the midst of as tragic interruptions as ever befell the writing of comedy anywhere.

With this lifelong habit of swift workmanship upon me, I thought that all I needed was to see my theme before me, and to go at it with my whole heart as I would have done at a new novel. In writing a novel you want a live place and live people; and these being provided, your book is as good as finished when you are half-way through with it. But I shall never forget in what a quagmire I landed myself when I began to write 'Chums' upon this principle. I have always, since I can remember, been a student of the acted drama. I acted for some years as dramatic critic in the provinces and in London. I knew as much about the exigencies of stage construction as the average man, and found that that meant a little less than nothing. The very method of work looked curiously bare and bald. My study for years has been to me a theatre in which I have acted many scores of different parts, often enough before a mirror to assure myself of nature. Yet I no sooner began to write consciously for the stage than this useful faculty abandoned me entirely. I no longer saw my living people; but in their stead the members of the travelling company obtruded themselves upon me.

My leading lady was before me in the place of Lucy Draycott. She was and is a most excellent and charming actress; but she was only playing at being Lucy Draycott, and she stood in between me and my own conception in a way which filled me with a cold embarrassment. Then, again, Square Jack Furlong, a rustic rascal, who, as I boldly hoped, was to make quite a new type of stage villain, was to be impersonated by a heavy man of quite the conventional sort—a man who (small blame to him) would have no idea of the accent my scoundrel was to speak in (a vital point to me) and not a conception of the inner workings of his mind. In this way all the real people who supposed they were to interpret my shadows into flesh and blood converted my flesh and blood into shadow. Understand that I am not apologizing for a bad play or a failure. It was not counted either one or the other, though I must do something different to touch the mark I am in quest of. I am only trying to show in what fashion I was embarrassed by new conditions. My travelling manager nearly broke his heart because I would not at first consent to allow my villain to shoot little Harold, and at last in desperation I took his advice and killed an idyll with a single grain of melodrama.

The piece was somehow written in the time prescribed, and was produced 'under the direct supervision of the author,' by which fact it gained perhaps as much as might have been expected. It was produced at Auckland, and achieved a success which it was not destined to repeat in its fulness. It was admirably, and in one respect originally, staged. The second act was laid in the New Zealand bush: and since at Auckland folks know what a New Zealand bush-scene is like, it was needful to be a little truer to nature than we found it easily possible to be when the play was produced for a single experimental night at the Globe, or when it ran its twelvemonth course in the English and Scotch provinces later on.

Sir George Grey was interested in the production; and in Auckland Sir George Grey does pretty much as he likes, as he has a right to do when one remembers what the city, and indeed the whole colony, owes to his patriotism, his statesmanship, and his personal generosity. Without his aid the stage-manager's proposal could not possibly have been carried out; but, armed with his authority, I presented myself to the curator of the park, and from him obtained leafage enough to dress the whole scene without the help of the scene-painter's art. We had a backcloth, to be sure, and an artificial waterfall (which flooded the cellars, by-the-by), but for everything else we were indebted to Sir George Grey and pure nature. The live bush, the wounds of the woodman's axe concealed by heaps of vari-coloured mosses, bloomed and rustled under the limelight as I suppose it never bloomed and rustled elsewhere in the history of the theatre, and the stage was ankle-deep in withered leaves; the scent of the forest actually getting beyond the footlights for once in a way.

I have never in my life seen any theatrical

spectacle one-half as lovely ; and this one scene had a great deal to do with the success of the piece. It was frantically applauded, and the scene-painter walked in front and bowed as if he had been responsible for its beauties. I overheard from a sun-tanned gentleman in the dress circle near whom I sat one useful trifle in the way of criticism. When Mr. Stuart Willoughby entered with his swag on his shoulder my neighbour whispered to *his* neighbour that *that* fellow had never learned to hump his bluey in Otago. 'I'll bet my head,' he added, 'that chap's an Australian.' And so he was. The future Stuart Willoughbys were instructed in this particular, and the most critical New Zealander could have found no fault with the style in which Mr. David James, junior, carried his belongings in the Otago bushland of the Globe Theatre, London.

'Chums' hit the New Zealand fancy, and the little play was kindly received in many places. I had begun to write another drama of a much more serious sort, and was working pretty busily as well at a revised edition of my first effort, when a serious accident befell us. My manager and I were travelling together to Dunedin (for we had formed a definite scheme of partnership, and had arranged to spend a year or two in the preparation of a *répertoire* of pieces which might be fit to face the lights of London by the time we got there), when a telegram found us at a railway station *en route*. It told us that an important member of the company had seceded. I know now the story of his secession; but I have some slight acquaintance with the law of libel, and the history is of no particular interest to anybody.

We were announced to open in Dunedin in 'Jim the Penman,' and our missing man was to have played the part of Baron Hardfeldt. The town was billed, seats were booked; there was no going back from the engagement without disaster. Then I had a goodly number of friends in Dunedin who were coming to see my own play, and there was a financial loss to be encountered into the bargain. Personally I experienced a keen sense of disappointment; but the manager was in despair. There was no filling the place of the recalcitrant for love or money—there was very little capital behind the concern; and, in short, it looked as if we had found a finish for our enterprise. Then it was that I bethought me, 'Why the dickens shouldn't I play Baron Hardfeldt?'

I communicated my idea to my companion, who grasped at it as a drowning man grips a straw. We consulted together. We found it possible to begin to study at midnight, and we arranged for a rehearsal on the morrow. I had seen the piece once, and recalled its general tenor, and began to construct a Hardfeldt. One of my dearest friends is a Züricher, and I felt certain of his accent. That was a point gained, for the rascally Baron might as well have come from Zürich as from anywhere else in the world. I recalled, with no twinge of inward apology, every tone of my old friend's voice, every trick of facial expression, and every little touch of Swiss gesture which helps his breezy and warm-hearted talk. I determined to dower Sir Charles Young's admirable scoundrel with all my dear old J—— G——'s tricks and manners; and I was the less remorseful in copying his cheerful and child-like *bonhomie* because our recalcitrant had been in the habit of giving the Baron away at his very entrance, and had stamped him from the first as a ruffian of the deepest dye, whereas I was disposed to think that a really successful adventurer would be likely to have an honest and engaging manner.

At midnight I began to study; and at three o'clock in the morning I went away to bed, carrying with me the words and business of the part and a pretty bad headache. We rehearsed at eleven; and I was 'letter-perfect,' as actors say, and was always to be found on the very nail of the stage on which I was wanted. I have always boasted a verbal memory like a steel rat-trap. It never lets anything go upon which it once seizes. So far excellent. 'But Linden saw another sight' at night-time. I knew platform fright as well as anybody. I have thrice been physically sick before addressing a strange audience, though I have been hardened by nearly a quarter of a century of practice. John Bright once said in my hearing that he never arose to speak in public without a feeling of insecurity at the knees and 'the sense of a scientific vacuum behind the waistcoat.' But this first appearance on the boards took me beyond anything I had hitherto experienced. I recalled the phrase about the 'scientific vacuum' which had fallen from the lips of England's greatest orator, and tried to console myself with the hope that I might not play so very vilely in spite of the fact that I had forgotten every line and word. I was bathed in a coward sweat whilst I stood near the central doors of the stage-chamber into which I was shortly to walk like a sheep to the slaughter. The cue came, and I entered mechanically crushing an opera-hat against my shirt-front. I know that if the audience could have seen the face below the grease-paint and the powder, they would have seen something very like the face of a corpse.

Luckily I am very short-sighted, and the space beyond the yellow glare of the footlights was no more than a black and empty gulf to me. The Penman, my miserable sin-steeped confederate, took me by the hand and introduced me cordially to Mrs. Ralston. Until he had ceased to speak I had no remotest idea of what I had to say; but the words came somehow, and I half fancied that my old friend J—— G—— had spoken them. There was a scattered round of applause at the end of the simple words I had to speak; for some of my friends in front had recognised me, as they might easily do, since I wore my own hair and beard. I did not think of this, but wondered dimly that I should have begun to make an impression so very early in the evening. I could see my breath rising like steam against the darkness of the auditorium, for it was cold weather and there was a touch of frost thus early even in the theatre. I sat and talked in dumb-show with Lady Dunscombe, was fittingly snubbed by Lord Drelincourt, and at length found myself alone with my confederate. The scene before me I knew to be one of the strongest of its class in the whole range of modern drama. I knew, impotent as I was, that I *could* play it —I could feel the sense of power tingling through my own impuissance. But the first essential was to know the words, and never a word knew I. Luckily Jim the Penman was an old stager, had played the part some two or three hundred times, and so knew most of the Baron's lines.

Whilst we were having our dumb talk with

Percival I had told him that my head was as empty as a blown egg-shell, and had fairly frightened him into taking care of me. He gave me my first words in a guarded whisper at the close of every speech of his own, and shepherded me with the utmost care through the whole scene. I shall never forget the well-meaning feeble villain, stricken down by remorse and impending terror, and the dominative Baron bullying him the while, with words supplied piecemeal by the sufferer.

'And vot haf you to do vith shame?' inquired the Baron, and there stuck. 'Wife you cherish,' whispered the denounced one; and, thus primed, the inexorable Baron resumed, and, having reached 'Wife you cherish,' stuck again. 'Children you adore,' whispered Jim the Penman, gazing upward at his tyrant with filmy eyes of suffering.

'And the children you adore,' echoed the Baron in a tone which spoke his unrelenting nature. At last came one intolerable, awful moment, when the hopeless Jim could prompt no longer. The prompter was at his post, but took no earthly notice of the scene. He had witnessed the rehearsal and was taking things easily. There was nothing else for it. I walked across to him and asked him for the line, received it, and spoke it with a biting scorn which nipped my confederate to the quick. I was congratulated on that unwilling walk across the stage afterwards by an old hand who was present at this first appearance of mine. He told me that the pause, the walk, the turn, and the indignant scorn with which the words were spoken had impressed him greatly, and had assured him that I was a born actor. But by that time I had found the courage of desperation, and all my fears had melted into thin air. The words of the subsequent acts came readily, and before the last curtain fell I was as much at home as I had ever found myself on the lecture platform.

XI

AMONGST actors one finds some of the queerest people in the world. The men of the modern school are very much like other people; but the old stagers can still find some of their number who are as richly comical as Mr. Vincent Crummles himself. They are like the dyer's hand, subdued to what they work in. I was thrown a great deal into the society of one elderly young gentleman whose speciality had for years been that sort of high-flying rattling comedy of which Charles Mathews was the chief exponent in my youth. He had the most suasive, genial, and gentlemanly comedy manner conceivable, and was never for a minute away from the footlights. At breakfast, at luncheon, at dinner, he played to the public of the hotel coffee-room. In the street he played to his fellow-promenaders. He played, and played hard, in the simplest private conversation. He had no more sense of moral responsibility than a butterfly. He was as admirable a stage liar, or nearly, as Mr. Hawtrey is; and off the stage he was as free from the trammels of veracity as he was when on it. He could promise, explain, evade, as dexterously in his own person as in the character of Lord Oldacre or Greythorne or Hummingtop. The world to him was literally a stage, and all the men and women merely players. Old age will teach him no sadness. He will play at being old. Death will have none of its common terrors for him. He will play at dying. When last I heard of him I was told that he was very, very poor; but I am sure he suffers little. He is playing at making a fortune or playing at having lost one: pluming himself on some visionary splendour, or commiserating some picturesquely broken nobleman in his own person.

I enjoyed the most astonishing adventure of my lifetime with this gentleman's aid, and by his express invention. He had secured the right to perform a play of mine through the Australasian colonies and through India. Of course there were certain pecuniary obligations attached to the matter, and, these being disregarded, I ventured into the theatre with a request for a settlement. My comedian was not in a position to effect a settlement, or perhaps he did not care to do it. He found a way out of the difficulty which I do not think would have occurred to one man in a million. He got rid of his creditor by giving him into custody for trespass; and I, being marched off by the police, had to find bail until the case was heard next morning. The magistrate advised me that I had a legal remedy; but my gentleman disbanded his company and betook him to a neighbouring colony. I was incensed at the time, though the business is laughable enough now, and I took out a writ against him, but never succeeded in serving it. When I had found my bail (a local editor was kind enough to pledge his word to save me from durance), I had to put in an appearance at the police station. There was a big policeman on duty there, and he went through the essential technicalities with so grave a face that the farce for a moment seemed quite real.

'What's your name?' asked the big policeman.

I told him, and spelled it for him.

'Your age?'

I answered that question also.

'What trade are you?'

'I am a man of letters.'

'What's that?'

'Man of letters. Write it down. Man—of—letters.'

'Are y' educated? Can ye read and write?'

I was flippant enough to say that I could read and write a little, and the big policeman entered me as being imperfectly educated. That record stands against me unto this day.

We played all through the principal towns, and then we took to bush-whacking, setting up one or two night stands in places rarely visited by a theatrical company; and I believe that the business done in these small places was almost always highly satisfactory from a monetary point of view. Some of the villages we visited—for they were nothing more—yielded fuller houses and realised better profits than we found always in the capitals. I remember that we played once in a schoolroom built of corrugated iron and without a vestige of scenery. We put on 'Chums;' and the settler's parlour, the forest scene, and the outer view of the Otago homestead were each and all represented with the help of a green baize cloth, which hung at the rear and on either side of the stage, three upturned petroleum tins, three chairs, a tub, and a little oblong deal table with red legs. We had a stage space of about four yards by three. I played Square Jack Furlong; and in the last act my revolver hung fire and exploded a second or two too late, when it was unfortunately and accidentally levelled at the back of the leading man's head. The waxen pellet which packed the powder hit him smartly on the philoprogenitive bump, and he swore audibly.

A revolver is always a nuisance on the stage and a terror to the actor who has to use it. You may buy the best weapon in the trade, you may have your cartridges made with the utmost care; but there will always be a chance of its missing fire. You may have a double in the wings, of course, but even that provides no surety. I have known my own revolver and the double refuse duty at the same instant, and have faced the moaned inquiry of the leading man, who ought to have been stretched out in apparent death throes, 'What the devil's going to happen now?' To make matters better, when I had thrown away the useless weapon with an improvised execration and was about to hurl myself upon the virtuous victim, the pistol in the wings obeyed the pressure of the prompter's finger, and the leading man dropped to a shot from nowhere, to the great mystification of the audience.

I am really disposed to believe that the illusion of the scene is very little helped by the most elaborate and realistic works of scene-painter, carpenter, and upholsterer. I have seen the house drowned in tears over that lugubrious and hollow 'East Lynne' when the stage has been enclosed in green baize and there has not been a stick of respectable furniture on the boards. 'East Lynne,' by the way, is one of my puzzles. Except that it has once or twice wearied me to the point of exasperation, it has never moved me in any way; and countless thousands have cried over it. In the New Zealand back blocks people used to weep like watering-carts over its tawdry pathos; and when that awful, awful child, whose business it was to die and who would *not* do his business, talked to his mother about his mamma, the handkerchiefs waved everywhere, and a chorus of sympathetic sniffings and throat clearings almost drowned the fustian rubbish of the dialogue. I played Lord Somebody in the piece one night. I forget the unreal wretch's name; but he will be remembered as taking money to Isabel. He appears in one scene only and has some twenty or thirty lines to speak; but he contrives to go further and oftener away from nature than any stage person whose acquaintance I have practically made. Nothing but the good old-fashioned 'moo-cow' style could possibly have suited him. I believe I can boast a tolerable imitation of that antiquated elocutionary method, and I certainly spared no effort.

'And you, Isabel, the daughter of an earl! how have you fallen!'

That is one of the gems of the old humbug's speech, and I mouthed it as it was made to be mouthed. The house took the burlesque with perfect seriousness and good faith—chiefly, I suppose, because it was impossible to make the vulgar rant too claptrappy and stagy. But as I was leaving, and as the house was already in a roar of applause, I came to grief. There was a dreadful draught at the back of the stage, and one of the ladies had been so careful against it as to pin the green-baize linings of the stage together so as to leave no place for an exit; and I was compelled to grope about for a minute or two in search of a way of escape whilst the applause changed to boisterous laughter.

And the memory of that little incident

helps me to a reflection on one detail of the actor's art which is more effective when fitly used, and more disastrous when neglected, than any other of the multitudinous things he has to know and to bear in mind. An exit is half the business of the most important scene ever written. You may play like an angel, you may hold the stage for half an hour and thrill your audience; but, after all, you may kill your supremest efforts by getting off clumsily. I write, of course, for the ignorant. The actor knows these things, and more than I can teach him into the bargain. But I had a singular instance of the fact in my own experience. It came early and gave me a lesson to be laid to heart. I never played before a more friendly audience. Good reports had gone ahead, and the house was willing, and I think was even eager, to be pleased. I had settled to that bright and happy confidence which is the actor's most blissful experience in comedy.

I think I never played so well in my life as in that first act of 'Jim the Penman;' but the stage was vast in comparison with any on which I had until then appeared, and my customary business brought me only within half a dozen paces of the door-way by which I should have vanished. A sudden sense of strangeness and constraint came down upon me like a cloud. The happy feeling of confidence vanished in a whiff of chill spiritual wind. The last line was spoken before that unhappy half-dozen of paces was achieved; and I left the stage in a dead silence, which was as eloquent of failure as it had been one brief minute earlier of success. I played half as well next night, but disappeared with *aplomb*, with an effect as encouraging as the most exigent artist could demand. So painful a thing is it to learn a new trade! 'So much to learn, so much to do!'

I am ready to propound a novel theory, and I am insolent enough to believe that I illustrate it in my own person. The time of full middle-age is that at which a man most readily adapts himself to a new art. It is at that time most assuredly necessary to accept certain physical limitations. I advise no hitherto unpractised person to seek excellence as a ground and lofty tumbler after five-and-forty. No sensible person who has attained that respectable altitude of years will try to make a *début* as Romeo. But supposing that a lad of fifteen and a man of five-and-forty begin on the same day to study landscape-painting, which of the two do you think will get nearer Nature's secret in five years' time? Personally I shall back—*cæteris paribus*—the man of middle age. Or if it come to acting, who is likely (physical limitations on both sides duly considered, of course) to offer you the better study of a bit of human nature—the matured observer or the unpractised unregarding youth? I back the middle-aged man once more.

My friendly critics of the London press told me that a middle-aged man had taken to the stage as a duck takes to water. It was a bit of kindly nonsense. I had worked like a galley-slave for nine months, and the nine months of a man of the world is worth the nine years of a boy. And do I profess to be an actor now? Not a bit of it, my friendly critic—not a bit of it, in all honesty. But I mean to be. There is no art so difficult—granted; but there is none so enchanting, so inspiring. Night after night for a whole week, bar Saturday, when Nature took a late revenge, I left a sick-room at Newcastle-on-Tyne; and every ache and pain fell away, and the sick treble changed to a healthy baritone, and manly strength came to pluck the halting pace of the invalid to marching time, and a feebly intermittent pulse grew full and calm at the splendid all-compelling influence of the stage. Had it been a cold lecture, now, or a speech on politics— and no man loves that kind of exercise more than I—the armchair and the warm fireside had not reached to me and beamed on me in vain. But the stage? That was another matter altogether. It is a better stimulant than the society of old friends. It is a finer anodyne than tobacco. It is a quicker and more constant pick-me-up than champagne. Sternest duty and purest pleasure wear one smiling face. And to think that I was well into the forties before I guessed this splendid truth!

But Nature is compensatory in everything, and her balance works in this accessible fairyland as elsewhere. The stage is the natural home of petty *contretemps*. When a man has dared to play in a piece of his own writing in a city like London it would be absurd to affect modesty or a want of belief in his own power to please. If under such conditions a man had no such faith, he would be an ass beyond the reach of satire. What else but faith in himself should bring him there? 'Que diable faisait-il dans *cette* galère?' Yet the bold amateur intruding is conscious of a resemblance in himself to the demons mentioned in Holy Writ. He believes (in himself), but he trembles.

The night of the tentative production of 'Ned's Chum' at the Globe Theatre was the brightest in my earthly calendar. Yet as I waited for my first cue an irresistible, horrible cold nausea got hold of me, and I had to fly back to my dressing-room and to endure on dry land all the agonies of *mal de mer*. The call-boy's warning cry slew one keen anguish with another, and the wretch who had been physically sick with fear a minute before was, under fire, as cool as a cucumber. But there came one moment more of heroic trial before the play was over. I keep religiously the notices of that first night, and I have laughed more than once at the gentle trouncing I got at the hands of Mr. William Archer in the columns of the *World*. My critic complained, tenderly enough, that at one point I took the stage with an obvious effort, as if determined to show that thus and thus should a man behave under sudden news of irreparable ruin. I cannot quite tell, said Mr. Archer in effect, why it was not admirable acting, and yet it was not. If he could have told, he went on to say, he might himself have been an excellent actor, and not a critic. But he wanted something—something was missing.

The miserable fact was this. I had never worn a wig in the part until that night, and I had forgotten for a mere instant that I wore one then. It was a part of the stage business to dash my wideawake hat to the ground, and—the wig came with it. For two or three dreadful seconds I stood frozen, expectant of the howl of laughter which generally follows such an accident. But the fates were kind, and the thing passed unnoticed save by two or three. My natural hair was much of the length and colour of the wig, and no derisive roar sounded in my ears. But I shall never forget the horror of those few waiting seconds; and I should like to ask Mr. Archer how far in his judgment such an occurrence might excuse an actor's momentary absence from pure nature.

I was once hit in the eye by a fragment of half-sodden turf thrown up by the explosion of a shell, and had time to think myself a dead man before I realised what had happened. On one occasion, his Excellency Ibrahim Pasha threatened to hang me out of hand; and I believed he meant to do it. I have been in many awkward corners in my time; but my inward forces were never more thoroughly routed than by that episode of the lost wig on the stage of the Globe Theatre.

XII

I suppose the confession I am about to make will stamp me in the minds of a great many people as an irredeemable barbarian. I care little for that, however, and I am staunch in the opinions which I have held all my lifetime. Perhaps my voice may find an echo here and there.

I am a lover of the noble art of self-defence, and to my way of thinking few greater blunders have been made by those who legislate for our well-being than was fallen into by the moral people who abolished the Prize-Ring. It should be admitted at once that the Ring was full of abuses at the time at which an end was made of it; but it was not beyond mending, and a marked deterioration has been noticeable in the character of our people since the sport of the Ring ceased to be a source of popular amusement. British fair play was a proverb amongst the roughest. The rules of the game were recognised even in a street fight, and the man who broke them was likely to be roughly handled.

It matters little that the sense of honour was crude and rough. It was there, and all bullies and blackguards were compelled to abide by it. So long as it was the fashion to fight with fists, the use of the knife, the bludgeon, and the brickbat was far rarer than it is now. The most ignorant crowd could be trusted to police a brace of combatants. There is no harm in a stand-up fight with the weapons of nature. Men *will* fight, and we English people had the least harmful way of fighting of all the peoples of the world. No man was ever good for much with his hands who was not chaste and temperate in life. Excellence in this pursuit was the growth of all the more masculine virtues.

I have the kindliest memories of some of the old heroes. The very first man who helped me on with a pair of boxing-gloves was the mighty 'Slasher'—the Tipton Slasher, William Perry, who in the days of my nonage kept the Champion of England public-house in my native parish of West Bromwich, in South Staffordshire. He it was who trained my youthful hands to guard my youthful head; and I have a foolish stupid pride and pleasure in the memory of that fact.

The Worcester and Birmingham Canal divides the parishes of Smethwick and West

Bromwich, and the Slasher's house was the last on the right-hand side—a shabby, seedy place enough, smoke-encrusted on the outside and mean within, but a temple of splendour all the same to the young imagination. The Champion of England dwelt there—the unconquered, the undisputed chieftain of the fighting clan. He reigned there for years, none daring to make him afraid.

I have been soundly flogged time and time again for visiting him. I have been put on bread and water and held in solitary confinement for the same misdemeanour, but the man had a glamour for me and drew me with the attraction of a magnet. I can see him now, almost as plainly as if he stood before me. He was a Hercules of a man, with enormous shoulders, and his rough honest mid-England features had a sort of surly welcome in their look. But for an odd deformity he would have had the stature of a giant; but he was hideously knock-kneed, and his shamble when he walked was awkward to the limits of the grotesque. You have only to invert the letter V to have an image of the Slasher's legs from foot to knee. His feet were strangers to each other; but his knees were inseparable friends, and hugged each other in a perpetual intimacy. In fighting he used to await his man, propped up in this inverted V fashion, and somehow he gained so solid a footing in that strange and clumsy attitude that he never, in all his experience of the Ring, received a knock-down blow until he encountered Tom Sayers in that last melancholy fight which cost him the championship, and the snug little property in the Champion of England public-house, and his friends and his reputation, and all he had in the world.

I earned one of the soundest thrashings I ever got in my life by playing truant from school in order to follow the Slasher to a wretched little race meeting, held at a place called The Roughs, on the side of the Birmingham Road, in the parish of Handsworth. My hero was there in glory, followed about by an innumerable tag-rag and bobtail, and I am afraid that on two occasions at least he was tempted to swagger and 'show off,' as children say. He shambled up to one of the 'try your strength' machines: the figure of a circus clown, with a buffer to punch at in the neighbourhood of his midriff, and a dial on his chest to indicate the weight of the blow administered. The Slasher tossed a penny to the proprietor of the machine and waved him on one side; but the man stood in front of the contrivance and besought him pathetically not to strike.

'Not you, Mr. Perry,' he said humbly; 'oh, not you, Mr. Perry.'

The Slasher, with an 'Away, slight man' motion of the hand, said 'Gerrout!' and the fellow obeyed, seeing that there was nothing else for it. Hercules spat upon his hand, clenched his fist, and smote. Crash went the whole machine into ruin, the wooden upright splintered, and the iron supports doubled into uselessness. The destroyer rolled on rejoicing; but the crowd made a subscription, and the owner of the machine stowed away his damaged property well pleased.

Mr. Morris Roberts was a gentleman known to local fame in those days—I am writing of five-and-thirty years ago—and Mr. Morris Roberts had a boxing-booth on the ground. In front of the booth he had a little platform, and from it he addressed the congregation gathered together at the beating of a gong.

'Walk up, gentlemen ; walk up, and see the noble art of self-defence practised by Englishmen, not like the cowardly Frenchman or I-talian, as uses sticks, knives, pistils, and other firearms, but the wepons pervided by nature. I've got a nigger inside as won't say No to no man. Also George Gough, as has fought fifteen knuckle fights within the last two years, and won 'em all, one man down and the next come on. If there's any sportsman here as cares to 'ave a turn at him, there's half-a-crown and a glass of sperrits for the man as stands before George Gough five minutes, no matter wheer he comes from.'

The Slasher, in the full tide of his wicked humour, stood below, and when the oration was ended he threw his old silk hat upon the stage. Mr. Morris Roberts was bawling that twopence did it—a first-rate sample of the noble art was to be seen for twopence—when this unexpected action froze him in mid-torrent.

'Come, come, Mr. Perry,' he said, when he had recovered himself a little, 'you can't expect George to stand up again the Champion of all England. That doesn't stand to reason, that doesn't. Now, does it, Mr. Perry?'

The Slasher smiled. 'All right. Hand down half a crown and that there glass o' sperrits.'

'You don't mean it, Mr. Perry,' said Mr. Morris Roberts.

'Don't I?' cried the Slasher.

A sudden inspiration illumined Mr. Morris's mind. 'All right. Come up, Mr.

Perry. Sixpence—sixpence—sixpence does it!'

It was no sooner known that the Champion was really resolved on business than the entrance to the booth was besieged. I was borne in breathless, all the wind being squeezed out of my small body by the pressure of the crowd, and bang went sixpence, the one coin which was to see me through the expenses of the day. It turned out that Mr. Gough had been impertinent to the Slasher, and the offended dignitary punched him, as I thought, a little unmercifully. At the close of the first round the man of the booth said—truthfully enough, no doubt—that he had had enough of it, and the entertainment came to a premature end.

That was the last I saw of the Slasher for years. He was the cynosure of all eyes then, and observed of all observers. But there is no wolf so strong but he may find another to make wolves' meat of him; and Tom Sayers, who had fought his first fight—so tradition tells—on the canal bank within a mile of the Slasher's public-house, sent in his challenge, and poor old Tipton's colours were lowered for once and for ever. He mortgaged the stock and goodwill of the house and backed himself for every penny he was worth, and he was beaten. He was grey and over-fat, and his fighting days were over. I forget now for how many years he had held the Championship Belt, but he ought to have been left to rest upon his laurels, surely.

He was dying when I saw him again, and his vast chest and shoulders were shrunken and bowed, so that one wondered where the very framework of the giant man had fallen to. He was despised and forgotten and left alone, and he sat on the side of his bed with an aspect altogether dejected and heartless. In his better days he had liked what he used to call 'a stripe of white satin,' which was the poetic for a glass of Old Tom gin. I carried a bottle of that liquor with me as a peace-offering, and a quarter of a pound of bird's-eye. He did not know me, and there was no speculation in his look; but after a drink he brightened. When I entered the room he sat in he was twirling an empty clay with a weary listless thumb and finger, and the tobacco was welcome.

'They mought ha' let me aloon,' he told me, when his wits grew clear, 'I'd held the belt for seventeen 'ear.' (I think he said seventeen, but 'Fistiana' is not at hand, and I can but make a guess at memory.) 'They mought ha' let me aloon. Tum's a good un. I've sin 'em all, an' I've niver sin a better. But he owed to ha' let me be. Theer was no credit to be got in hommerin' a man at my time o' life. All the same, mind ye, I thowt I should ha' trounced him. So I should if I could ha' got at him; but he fled hither an' he fled thither, and he was about me like a cooper a-walkin' round a cask. An' I was fule enough to lose temper, an' the crowd begun to laugh an' gibe at me, an' I took to räacin' round after him, an' my wind went, an' wheer was I then? He knocked me down—fair an' square he did it. Th' on'y time it iver chanced to me. I put everythin' I had o' that fight, an' here I bin.'

It will be within the memory of such as care for these things that, after the last great battle which brought the fistic history of England to a glorious close, Tom Sayers and the Benicia Boy, his late opponent, enlisted with Messrs. Howes and Cushing, proprietors of a circus in those days, and travelled the country, sparring nightly in amity together. My father, who had naturally about as much sympathy with the Prize-Ring as with the atrocities of the King of Dahomey, was nevertheless fired with admiration for the hero of Farnborough, and must needs go to see him. He astonished everybody who knew him by showing his silver head and whiskers in the bar parlour of the hotel at which Mr. Sayers was quartered for the night. I suppose that the worshippers at Tom's shrine were of another sort as a rule; but he was evidently and mightily impressed by the old gentleman's interest in his career. He told a story which, in its main lines, I remember as well as if I had heard it yesterday, though I rack my brains in vain for the names of the two people concerned in it.

'I suppose, sir,' said Tom, 'as you never heard how I come to fight'—let me call him Jones.

No, my father never had heard.

'Well, it was like this. Lord —— comes to me a week or two before the Derby, and "Tom," he says, "I've got a notion. You and me," he says, "is goin' down to the Derby together," he says. "I've got a pair of snow-white mokes," he says, "and I've bought a coster's shallow. I'm having it painted white and picked out in gold," he says, "and it's going to be upholstered in white satin. Now, you and me, Tom," says his lordship—"you and me's going to get up in white shoes, white kickseys, white westcuts, white hats, white coats, white ties, and white gloves," he says. "We'll go down a reg'lar pair of bloomin' lilies!" Well, we did, and it was agreed to be the best turn-out of the day. We was walkin' in the ring when up comes Jones, and, without with your leave or by your leave, he hits me on the nose. Well, I was that soft and out of condition the clarrit was all over me in no time. I was goin' for Jones like a shot; but his lordship he stops me and he says, "Tom," he says, "you shall fight him," he says, "for two hundred pound." I did, and you may believe as I paid him out for that.'

We were greatly impressed with this narrative, and I have always thought the regular pair of blooming lilies delicious. I told Tom that I had known the poor old Slasher, and he spoke of him with respectful sympathy.

'He was the right sort, the Tipton was,

and I was sorry to take him down. Perhaps somebody 'll come one of these days and lower my colours. It's my turn to-day and somebody else's to-morrow.'

I vex the shades no more. Their form of valour is no longer known amongst us; but there are some who regret. I find pathetics among them, and quaint humours, in my memory.

THE END

www.ingramcontent.com/pod-product-compliance
Lightning Source LLC
Chambersburg PA
CBHW031826230426
43669CB00009B/1244